SOFT
SUCCULENTS

Aeoniums, Echeverias, Crassulas, Sedums,
Kalanchoes, and related plants

JEFF MOORE

Dudleya brittonii

This book is dedicated to all my regular and semi-regular customers that have kept my little nursery in Solana Beach open for the past 25 years. Hopefully I've lured you in with quality plants at a fair price and good advice. But I know there are a handful of you that, while you definitely are into the plants, probably spend money at my place at least partially because you like to see a small business succeed. The same plant might have been cheaper at Home Depot (if they had it). For that I thank you. And for those of you for whom I've served as an enabler for your addiction, well sorry, but I know it has brought you happiness, and you too have helped keep me in business. Now, please, read this book and expand your list of succulents you didn't know you needed.

CONTENTS

ACKNOWLEDGMENTS

The starting point for the information I've put forward in this book was from my own experience from 25 years of owning a succulent nursery. I thought I knew the subject well, which I kind of do, but I know it a whole lot better now after researching this book. I'm fortunate to have had the help of John Trager of the Huntington Library and Botanic Garden, Randy Baldwin of San Marcos Growers in Santa Barbara (and his informative and thorough website) and Bryan Kemble of the Bancroft Garden in Walnut Creek, CA. You wouldn't want to play Succulent Jeopardy with these guys. I'm also thankful to Nels Christensen, Viggo Gram, and Jeremy Spath for contributing some beautiful habitat images. I'd also like to acknowledge the help and advice from some of the 'plant people' I've done business with over the years, including Robin Stockwell, Debra Baldwin, Tom Jesch of Waterwise Botanicals, Ron Regehr, Brad Brown, Larry Weitzel, Dan Bach, Brent Wigand, Mark of B&B, Julian Duval, Kelly Griffin, Jeremy Spath, the Rojas siblings, Greg Vosper, Dick Wright, Tina Zucker, Patrick McMahon, Mark Reidler, Hans and family from Western Cactus.

Dudleya brittoni x pulverulenta

PREFACE

This is the third in what I hope will be a series of books about succulents in cultivation. My first book, *Under the Spell of Succulents*, took a broad overview of succulents in captivity, and the various ways we engage with them. One of my frustrations was how I could only offer a 5 or 10 page glimpse of some of the major plants in all the various genera – there was so much more to show and tell, but a book can only be so thick. So, with the modest success of that first book, I was able to fund and publish my second project, *Aloes and Agaves in Cultivation*. Now I'm focusing here on some of the most popular succulents – the various soft, fleshy and colorful plants that are probably most deserving of the term 'succulent'. There is nary a spine or anything even close to sharp on any of the plants featured in this book – indeed, you could take a dive into and roll around on any of these juicy creatures, and the only damage would be to the plants and maybe stains on your clothes. These softies will pass the nervous grandma test.

My first thought for this book was to call it 'Aeoniums and Echeverias', as those were the two primary genera I wanted to cover – and still do receive the most coverage here. But I wasn't sure there was a big enough market for just those two groups. And if I did that book, would I do a later book dedicated to sedums, crassulas, kalanchoes, etc.? Would there be enough of a market for that volume? How many books do I have in me? I slowly came around to the idea of a book dedicated to all the soft and gorgeous succulents so currently in favor. And although a majority of the genera here are from the broad crassulaceae family, that would be a misleading title, because the casual succulent aficionado associates that term with only the crassula genus, which resides within the larger crassulacaea family but is really only a small part of it. Since the succulents in this book have been included on the basis of looks, compatibility and 'feel' over proper botanical relationship, the best descriptive term I could come up with was 'soft'. Implicit in that term is a lack of spines or serrations, which is a characteristic of many succulents (which are often also 'soft' below their defensive armor). Plus, 'soft' is a nice, disarming term for those who associate succulents with 'cactus', and it kept the book title short and simple.

Most of the plants in this book are from Africa, Mexico or South America, although the dudleyas lay claim to being one of the few ornamental succulents from California and northern Baja. I've introduced most of the groups with some habitat images, and in the case of dudleyas, I might have more habitat images than cultivation shots, as their habitat is in my backyard and I've got some really nice images. But this book is primarily about how we grow these plants in cultivation. If you've read either of my previous books, I make it apparent that I'm addressing most of the cultural advice to my fellow Californians – which is where I live and the majority of succulent enthusiasts live. We've got it easy, but for any of you outside our climate reading this book, I hope you enjoy it as inspiration, and can find a way to play with succulents within the limitation of your climate and situation. Got a greenhouse?

For the most part, the beauty and color is more in the foliage than the flowers. If a particular plant or group offers exceptional blooms, they will be shown, but when the flower is not showy, I've chosesn to go with the best image of the plant – whether in bloom or not.

I hope you enjoy the images of all these little wonders. I took most of them with a Cannon G16 'point and shoot', and even a handful with an Iphone. These guys are great photo subjects, and they are just waiting there for you. You don't even have to sneak up on them. I also borrowed superior images from friends when available, particularly for the habitat shots. There isn't a whole lot of text offered beyond the introductory chapters, but what there is will be tips and observations from a life in the succulent nursery business. Thank you for taking an interest in my book and I hope it inspires you to get out there and have fun with succulents.

Order: Saxifagales

Family: Crassulaceae

Genus: Kalanchoe

Species: luciae

cv.: 'Fantastic'

INTRODUCTION

B y choosing 'soft succulents' as the title of this book, it should be apparent that I am selecting plants/genera based on appearance and physical characteristics, not necessarily upon botanical or Linnaean categories. Many of these plants are fairly easy to identify into the proper genus at a glance – at least once you've been around them for a while. Most aeoniums have similar rosettes of thin leaves with very tiny serrations and grow on stalks. But there is at least one, *Aeonium nobile,* that has such thick and fleshy leaves that I at first thought it was a type of echeveria. Sedums and crassulas are both very diverse genera, and it can be a challenge figuring out which group a certain bushy succulent belongs to (flowers can be a 'tell'). The mesemb group is huge and highly variable. Most have jelly-like or 'gumby'-like translucent leaves. Kalanchoes are also variable, some fuzzy, all soft and a bit delicate, with a few that don't really look like the rest of the family. The goal with this book is to give you an idea of what each group basically looks like, and identification will become easier over time.

If you're new to the world of succulent plants, be aware that 'succulent' or 'succulence' is just a descriptive term, and is not a botanical classification. Succulents are plants from dry climates that have evolved bodies (or leaves or roots) that store water to get them through dry times. There are some plant groups or families that are primarily not succulent, but have certain members that have slowly adapted to their particular climate as it became more arid, and are now what we can call 'succulent' in nature. This evolutionary adaptation can give them a plumpness that often has a visual appeal, or a unique architecture that helps them stand apart from the rest of the botanical world. They can run the gamut from cute and comical to staggeringly beautiful to strange to almost scary. There is a tremendous diversity in form within the succulent realm, yet after a while, you just know one when you see one. And for those of us that live within the proper climate (i.e. mediterranean), they are among the easiest of plants to keep alive. If you live where it gets too cold or too wet (or even too hot, believe it or not), you can still grow these as container plants in sunny windows or outdoors during the proper time of year, but not as year-round landscape plants.

The majority of plants featured can be found either in general or specialty nurseries, some more available than others. Some of the more rare succulents are so not due to the difficulty of keeping them alive, but because of the difficulty of propagating them into more plants. Single rosette, non-offsetting plants such as many dudleyas and some echeverias must be grown from seed, which can be a long and laborious project. Others are much easier. One of the most common plants in California is the 'jade', *Crassula ovata,* and I'm sure a large number of those weren't consciously planted;

a piece just fell and rooted where it landed. Even easier to propagate, and in fact becoming enough of a nuisance to be considered a succulent 'weed', are some of the 'mother of millions' forms of kalanchoe. These ambitious colonists simply grow hundreds (seems like millions) of baby plantlets on the leaf edges that fall and grow where they land, with roots already started. Succulents can be a lazy gardener's best friend.

From experience at my nursery, I know that there are quite a few 'anti spinites' that love succulents, but rule out any plant with anything resembling a sharp tip anywhere on the plant. Soft succulents are the only types of succulents they will consider buying (which pains me, because they are ruling out so many wonderful plants! See the discussion on the following pages). But there are just so many soft succulents on the market now, and even the word 'succulent' doesn't elicit the giggles it used to; people pretty much know we're talking about a category of plant.

Mesembs, stapeliads and cotyledons didn't immediately occur to me as candidates to be included in this book, but are predominantly soft and spineless, and while they might not always be prominent in the dish garden movement, they are nevertheless fantastic plants with sometimes stunning flowers, so I've included at least the most prominent and available plants of those genera.

Some of the more obscure, smaller succulent groups that fit the 'spineless, soft' category may be mentioned in passing only. For example, the adeniums (above left) are wonderful succulent 'fat plants' with glorious flowers, but they fall more into the collector category, not practical in the landscape or in group plantings. The same applies to dorstenias, fockeas, and many other rarities. Those types of succulents often have a more structural, stand-alone appeal. I'm hoping to dedicate a future volume to those type of plants, and if you bought this book, thank you – you're helping me fund the next project!

Although the plants featured here may be from different continents, and some are not even remotely related – other than belonging under the general and non-scientific umbrella of 'succulents' – most have a similar visual appeal, that of generally soft, colorful, mainly rosette shaped plants. The plants in this book just sort of belong in the same category, even if that defies Linnaean logic. They 'feel' like they belong in the same conversation – soft, fleshy, and colorful. Botanists might not see why a dudleya and kalanchoe belong in the same book, but enthusiast don't care about chromosomes. It is a visual thing for us.

The chapters about the plants to follow are genus classifications ('echeverias', 'aeoniums', 'sedums', etc . . . Each chapter will show some of the true species that are prominent in cultivation within each genus (*Echeveria colorata* for example). We'll also look at some cultivars of that species, which are still the same species, but have been isolated for some unique physical attribute (*Echeveria colorata* 'Mexican Giant'). In fact, in the case just mentioned the cultivar is more common in cultivation than the true species, which happens a lot. Prominent hybrids are major players with many of these plants as well, and will get equal time. There are likely more hybrid aeoniums in California than true species, and often what we think is a true species is actually a hybrid. Some of these hybrids were intentional creations, others just did it on their own and made their way into cultivation, either with an agreed upon name or not. There are also more hybrids within the echeveria and related groups than there are true species available, and for good reason – they are often visually superior plants. I've opted to show plants based upon popularity, availability and beauty over a 'species vs. hybrids' categorization. Most enthusiasts like to know the story behind their plants, but don't really care whether it is a true species or hybrid or cultivar – we just like them and want to know how to care for them.

In the introduction to each chapter, I'll give you an idea of where the group's native habitat is, but I've opted not to identify the native range of each individual species. As thorough as I want this book to be, I hate to defer to Google on this – but for further research, you can always, you know, Google it.

I highly recommend *Succulent Plants of the World* (Timber Press) by Fred Dotort to explore the plants herein further. Later in the book I'll recommend books dedicated to specific genera, but to my knowledge there isn't a user-friendly book dedicated to kalanchoes or stapeliads or some of the smaller groups. Dotort's book takes a broad overlook at them all, with excellent images. It focuses a bit more on habitat than cultivation, but overall it is an excellent and inspiring treatment of all the major succulent groups, excluding cacti. There are some fantastic images of plants that have rarely if ever made it into cultivation, but will make you hope they do soon.

One of the frustrations I had with my aloe/agave book was that there was no way I could include all the plants I wanted to into one book and keep it to a manageable size. I have run into that issue again here, as I knew I would. The goal is to show you the best, most prominent, and hopefully most available from each genus. There will be a few rarities that can give you something for your wish list. Some plants receive a single image, others an entire page or even a two page spread. Species or groups that get more space have received such because they are important and frequently encountered, or because I have a personal affinity for them (author's prerogative), or because I happen to have some extra nice images and I just had to use them. For further research, I hope you can locate some of the best books on the subject, and I've provided cover images here of quite a few, as you can see above. Some are out of print but are worth tracking down if you can.

So, where can you grow these primarily African, Mexican, and Canary Island plants? Well, besides the obvious answer of those places in particular, most soft succulents do

better in a mediterranean as opposed to desert climate, with a few exceptions. In the U.S., the easiest climate for these plants is California, from the Mexican border to the San Francisco bay area, from the coast to the foothills. The farther from the coast you get, the more some plants can be affected by summer heat or winter cold. The extra winter rain farther north can be great for some plants (aeoniums), difficult for many others. You might think a tropical area like Florida would be good for succulents, and it is for some, but many have a tough time. When I told Bill Branch from Fort Myers, Florida, that I was planning a book on these plants, he offered up his experience (see following page).

Not included in this book will be aloes and agaves (I already wrote a book about those – you should get it). Almost all agaves have wicked spines, but there is at least one exception, *Agave attenuata* – the 'Boutin's Blue' form is seen above right. Aloes tend to look spiny, although most have very benign serrations that won't draw blood, and a few, such as *Aloe striata*, above left, have completely smooth edges. There are even true cacti that are spineless, albeit often in aberrant forms, such as the 'Totem Pole', *Lophocereus schottii* v. monstrose, seen below left. In the normal, non-monstrose form, this same species is very spiny. There are also quite a few of the 'orchid' cacti, such as the famous 'Christmas cactus' or various epiphyllums, as well as some pereskias, that make a very weak attempt at forming anything resembling a spine or thorn. Below right is *Euphorbia leucodendron,* one of many euphorbias that lack spines. However, most euphorbias are more rigid in structure, and have a nasty white latex sap, which makes them not as friendly to play with as the plants featured in this book. I hope to cover them in a future volume.

So you sort of have to learn as you go which ones are easy for you and which aren't. Wherever you live, a good sunny window (some direct sun every day) usually works, which may get your plants through the winter. If you are really into it, you may want to have a heated greenhouse for half the year. Almost universally, these plants don't want to freeze and are adverse to snow or the conditions leading up to it.

I have owned a succulent nursery for 25 years, and there are still times that I'll look at a soft succulent, and not only will the name not pop into my head (this may be age related), but even the genus isn't immediately apparent. It could be a sedum, or a crassula, or something more obscure. This might be because my brain is at capacity for Latin plants names, but more likely because there are cases of convergent evolution and quite a few intergeneric crosses. Echeverias can be crossed with sedums to create sedeverias, or with pachyphytums to create pachyverias. There are graptosedums as well. Sometimes a grower will isolate a particular sport or cultivar (a visually unique individual plant), grow it on and propagate it, and give it its own cultivar name – sometimes through the proper channels, sometimes not. Or two different growers will do the same cross at different locations and times, and give the same plant two different names – and the plants might even look a little different. Different growers sometimes make up their own names even if a previously accepted name exists (I'm not naming names, but you know who you are). So don't feel bad if you're not sure exactly which plant you have; what's important is that you have it and you like it. You can properly identify it eventually. Maybe.

That last statement can be a sore spot for some plant collectors, but it's a reality. You can't trust general nurseries to always have succulents properly labeled. There are just too many varieties, and the growers that produce them don't always know some of the subtle differences of the many types and cultivars. The plant might come with a label that just says 'succulent' or maybe it gets a little closer and just gives you the genus. Unless you're buying from a succulent specialty nursery, you certainly can't expect the employees to know the entire succulent spectrum. And even those of us with succulent nurseries have to guess sometimes at the unlabeled plants we acquire. I'm hoping this book helps a little, but I'm quite sure some of the plants 'identified' herein will be the subject of dispute.

What exactly is a succulent? One thing to keep in mind is that the word is really just a description, and not by any means a type of Linnaean botanical classification. It just means 'juicy', and regarding plants, the word applies to those that hold water in their leaves, stems or roots. They do this because they are primarily from arid parts of the world where rain is infrequent, and plants from many different families and genera have evolved this survival mechanism as their habitat dried up over time. The most famous type of succulents are probably those from the cactus family, but as the term 'succulent' has become more known and accepted, it generally now applies to all succulent plants that are not cactus. The phrase 'Cactus and Succulents' is used often, even though that is technically redundant.

Top left: This little aeonium jungle greets visitors at Succulent Gardens in Watsonville, CA. I can't speak for the designer, but I bet this little slope started as a collection of 1-gallon plants, which just morphed in unexpected ways over time to create an eye-pleasing but not wholly expected composition of drifts and colors. Gardening can be a series of happy accidents.

Below left: A grower's flat of *Aeonim arboreum v. holochrysum* displaying seasonal tannic stripes.

Right: One of the geometrically 'stacked' crassulas, the dainty little *Crassula* 'caput minima'.

An unidentified dudlya, possibly *D. candida*. Don't think the tips are sharp. Dudleyas, like most plants in this book, can be easily crushed if you're not careful. This type of plant also has a thin white powdery covering that will leave fingerprints if touched. And it also doesn't like to be watered much. So just put it in the sun and leave it alone and it should be happy. I love nature. *Photo by Viggo Gram.*

Above is the beautiful but difficult to grow variegated echeveria called 'Compton's Carousel'.

If you've tried and killed a traditional bonsai tree, keep the pot and try a jade, such as *Crassula* 'Hobbit' at left. It has a natural tree-like shape and can live in a confined space.

Bottom: The variegated form of *Kalanchoe luciae* known as 'Fantastic', next to the rare *Dudleya pachyphytum*.

The research that I put into this book came at first from my own head (I've been doing this a while), but then I went to some of the more specific books in my plant library to double check and quite often found out I've been calling a plant by the wrong name for as long as I've known it. I also sent a lot of images off to some experts I know in the field for proper identification. Sometimes I'd head for the internet, which either confirmed what I thought was right, or muddied the waters even further. I don't think I'm telling you anything new when I say there is a lot of wrong stuff on the internet, sometimes very authoritative in its wrongness. There are also a lot of wonderful images online of plants that are almost impossible to find, or have been doctored to an extent that it might be a new species that only exists in cyberspace. I've seen quite a few frustrated customers on quixotic succulent Pinterest quests for plants they will likely never find, or if they eventually do, will find them impossible to grow.

As mentioned earlier, I have been in the succulent business a long time, but the process of making books over the past few years has really taught me how much I didn't know, or knew wrong, or knew partially. I have bounced some questions off of botanic garden or grower specialists that

know this field better than I do, and find some comfort that they are often equally frustrated or confused over something that was also giving me fits. Sometimes this was a result of improper or lost data regarding long-ago hybridization projects, or confusion over multiple common names being attributed to the same plant. John Trager, curator of the Desert Garden at the Huntington Library and Gardens knows more about these plants than almost anyone, and even he admits sometimes you just have to give it your best guess and let it go. Nature is indifferent to our man-made pigeon-hole classification systems.

A point I'll make more than once in this book is that there are some easily identifiable species, and then a whole bunch of crosses based off these primaries that make for some beautiful creations, but muddy the waters regarding identification. This is especially true with aeoniums and echeverias. Dick Wright did many of the early echeveria hybrids, and he said that after sprouting hundreds of seedlings on a first-generation cross, he would pick the best or strongest individual to name and further propagate (there is always variability in every seed batch), but then couldn't let himself destroy all the other slightly 'lesser' offspring, and would release them un-named

Beauty and the beast, or beauty and a different type of beauty if you're like me. The Jack Catlin hybrid aeonium provides an interesting contrast to the red glochid-spined *Opuntia rufida*. Both plants look inviting to the touch, but I'd only advise it for the aeonium. Totally different succulent plants from distant habitats, but both can live happily side-by-side in a mediterranean climate.

out to other growers or distributors. So the result would be a plethora of wonderful new echeverias that might almost be *Echeveria* 'Arlie Wright', but not quite the same, and never named. Hearing that made me feel better about my ignorance. So our goal here will be to help you understand and be inspired by these succulent beauties, hopefully get the name right or at least get close, and continue your own research if you are so inclined. I'll be watching my inbox for corrections, you perfectionists out there.

Having been a succulent enthusiast and nursery owner for a long time, I've always dealt with and enjoyed the various soft succulents, but my plant passion was always more towards aloes and agaves and some of the more structurally unique caudiciforms

Check out this magnificent malfunction. Sometimes succulents just do weird stuff. This is *Aeonium* 'Sunburst', which has a propensity to occasionally grow in the mutated crested or fasciated form. But typically the plant itself crests, not the flower as is the case here – at least that is what I think it is doing. Aeoniums are monocarpic bloomers, meaning this is an end-of-life phenomenon, so by the time you read this, this mutant flower will have long ago died off. Thank you Todd Setzer of Point Loma for sending me these images just before the book went to press.

There are a number of plants that can be described as semi-succulent, such as plumerias (I consider them a succulent despite their tropical appeal) and desert succulent trees such as burseras and commiphoras, or many of the cool-weather sedums that look succulent but really have higher water needs. One way to consider whether a plant is succulent: would it leave a wet spot if stepped on or run over? If so, it is likely a succulent. All of the plants in this book will leave a wet spot.

Above: The rarely seen but stunning flowers of a type of 'ice plant', *Ruschia lineolata*, which makes a nice, flat low-growing groundcover.

Below: some examples of convergent evolution with a series of unrelated 'flapjack' or 'clamshell' shaped plants. Left: *Cotyledon macrantha*. Middle: *Kalanchoe luciae*. Right: *Crassula arborescens*. Certain design templates seem to work efficiently in warm/dry climates. That would apply as well to the parallel spherical or columnar shapes of many cacti and euphorbias.

or crested plants. Putting this book together has really given me a much greater appreciation for these softer and colorful beauties, and it has opened up a new soft spot in my heart for soft succulents. Corny but true.

There are some examples of convergent evolution in the succulent realm. For example, there are some cacti that look a bit like euphorbias, or agaves that look like aloes – at least until your eye becomes more refined. My unrefined eye got me confused with the plant above, discovered unlabeled in a local landscape. My first guess was that it was a gray-green aeonium, but most aeoniums tend more to the green, with the gray-glaucous color scheme more evident in echeverias. As this seemed to be a low, tight clump, I figured it might be an echeveria. Then I discovered a plant from yet another genus, *Sedum pachyclados,* that looked a lot like this, although this one seemed to lack that plant's slight ruffle on the leaf edges. So how do you figure out which genus it belongs to? Wait until it blooms. A few months after taking the image above middle, I revisited the site and found it in flower. As you can see, entire rosettes are elongating into spring flowers in the monocarpic style of many of the other aeoniums in the same bed – so it is an aeonium. Which aeonium? That was as far as my detective work got me – I'm taking the easy way out and labeling it a hybrid.

This aim of this book is to be more encyclopedic and informative about the plants themselves than it is an 'arts and crafts', how-to/DIY about succulent arranging. However, as you'll see here and in the next section, these are those kind of plants, so plant combinations will be shown as much as space allows. It is a fun way to engage with succulents, and the contrasts and combinations can be quite stunning. Aside from traditional container gardens, enthusiasts are creating succulent murals, succulent baskets, succulent hats, pumpkins, shoes, just about succulent anything. I once had a customer get so carried away with her succulent project that she came into my nursery looking for a succulent that has uniform 3" rosettes, mauve-pink in color, small flowers ... she went on with the description, and I realized she wasn't talking about a plant she'd seen, it was some ideal plant that existed only in her imagination, but would really help her design. So she was into it more for the art than for the plants. Maybe someday someone will hybridize just what she's looking for, but in my opinion, the plant is the thing.

Topiary turtle by Samia Rose Topiary.

Above: a noble project gone awry, or in truth just drawn out to its inevitable conclusion. Succulent murals, tapestries or topiaries can be beautiful, but expensive and short-lived unless you are a maintenance fanatic. And the word 'maintenance' usually doesn't go well with the word 'succulent', as we succulent enthusiasts are usually spoiled by how little work they require. These types of projects are hampered by the difficulty of keeping them hydrated and nourished, as actual soil is either a minor component or not used at all. I spend a lot of time at my nursery trying to talk folks out of these projects (and talking myself out of sales money). But hey, if you've got the time, money and willingness to keep at it, by all means, have a go. Look how nice the big projects (used to) look on the facing page.

Right: a properly done vertical garden should look its best a month or two after planting, once the plants begin to happily crowd each other a bit. This particular arrangement stands a better chance than the one in the middle photo, as there are a series of angled pockets behind each plant, providing some soil for them to grow in.

Succulent wreaths are pretty cool. They are typically made by inserting bare-root cuttings into a meshed tube of moss, with a metal ring in back for structural support. They have to be planted densely to look good, with a nice variety, as seen above. They need a good amount of sun, a weekly soaking, and occasional trimming to keep them looking wreath-like, but there is a point where you have to give up. The owner of this wreath got two good years and then gave up a long time before the image below, but a lot of the plants refused to die. Even the wall paint has faded in that time. If you plant this old 'wreath' in soil, it will then become a big, happy, regenerated bowl of succulents.

Got cuttings? You'd need a boatload to build a succulent wall like the one below at Waterwise Botanicals in Bonsall, CA., or the succulent valentine above left at Succulent Gardens in Watsonville, CA. Vertical succulent gardens like these or the wreath at right can be fantastic expressions of an intersection of art and nature, but they have a limited shelf life. With proper

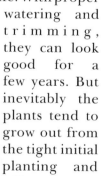

watering and trimming, they can look good for a few years. But inevitably the plants tend to grow out from the tight initial planting and will get leggy, as you can see in the neglected, 3-year old wreath below right. So there comes a point down the road when it is time to decommission the installation, and return the plants to pots or the ground so they can continue their lives in a more accommodating environment. Look at these projects as temporary art installations that serve as a source of future new cuttings.

CONTAINER GARDENS

Photo: Bob Wigand

Above: an entryway vertical pot shows the late stages of an aeonium bloom.

Above: this mini-landscape uses rocks to simulate boulders.

There are very few rules you need to follow when creating cornucopia containers. Most of the plants have the same requirements, but you should know which ones will stay miniature, and which really want to bust out and get big. You can keep a larger plant dwarfed in a small pot for a while, but it may end up crowding out its mates, or simply fail to thrive due to an inability to grow. For example, aloes or agaves might look perfect in a 4" starter size to pair with other mini succulents, but really should be grown long-term in larger pots or in the ground.

As with succulent landscaping, try not to make it too crowded right off the bat, as they need room to grow, although it can be satisfying to start right off with a full and finished-looking bowl, especially if it is a gift.

Most succulents are fine as solitary container plants, but many soft succulents seem like they were designed to be combined. Once an artistically inclined person discovers succulents, they soon find that even with a brown thumb they can create all manner of colorful combinations. You can draw a parallel with flower arranging when you put combination bowls together. Consider a vertical plant, a lower sculptural or bushy specimen, and a cascader. One cute way someone came up with to remember this concept is to think of a 'thriller, a filler, and a spiller'. Flowers will add color, but most succulents provide as much or more color in their year-round foliage. In the photo above, the large-flowered form of *Euphorbia milii* (also known as 'Crown of Thorns', but the thorns are fairly benign compared to cacti) is one of the few succulents that is in flower most of the year, but the rest of the color is just full-time foliage. Pots as full as these can usually crowd and grow together for several years before they need any thinning out.

Top right: a dense collection of sedums, crassulas, mesembs, and echeverias surround a blue columnar cactus. Below right: a tightly packed combination bowl of sempervivums, sedums and echeverias offers a subdued, somewhat monochromatic display. Top left: Senecios, crassulas and graptopetalums fill a small bowl. Below left: an abundant combination of colorful succulents in a giant clam knockoff bowl.

Tall, vertical planters can present a challenge to plant. Do you go with a tall plant, or cascading plants? Consider both, as seen here with an aeonium-themed tandem, including some cascading sedums and senecios.

Softies and Spinies

Soft and spiny succulents can work well together in containers. The old, long-established and maybe overgrown container at left has a 'Madagascar Palm' *(Pachypodium lamerei)* as the feature plant with Golden Barrel cacti *(Echinocactus grusonii),* and the blue graptopetalum providing a soothing contrast to the bright yellow.

Right: *Agave lophantha* 'Quadricolor' is an extraordinary small variegated agave that lends itself well to container culture, either singly, or in this case as the architectural element in an otherwise soft succulent bowl.

Succulents can be combined with non-succulents, providing those plants don't require too much water and can handle sun. In this case, *Echeveria* 'Afterglow' are complimented by winter-blooming cyclamen for a soft and cool-colored doorstep arrangement. As you might guess, after a period of time, the echeverias still looked fine, but the cyclamen began to go downhill, so the owner treated them as temporary bedding plants and put some different companion plants in their place.

Right: succulent handbags made of a porous planting material grace the side of a barn at Succulent Gardens in Watsonville, CA. You want some cascading succulents for these kind of plantings.

Below: a crowded cornucopia of compellingly combined crassulaceaens. C'mon, credit for cranial creativity.

One Plant / One Pot

Most of the containerized succulents you'll see in this book, and just in general, are planted in combinations, because it is fun and cool and colorful and you can get so creative and almost paint with them. However, for those of us who are a bit more into the 'plant is the thing', botanical way of appreciating plants, having a pot dedicated to a single plant/species sometimes gives you a greater appreciation of that individual. This is especially true for collector specimen plants that are so unique and/or rare that you don't want any companion or competition neighbor in the pot. But even some of the more common succulents that are more typically seen in the company of others, such as the aeonium hybrid below or the *Sedum clavatum* above right, deserve individual attention for their wonderful architecture.

Aeonium 'Catlin hybrid'

Most serious collectors, or those with more of a botanical than artistic bent, will usually keep their plants singly, in the 'one-plant, one-pot' mode. This is particularly true when the plant appeals as a stand-alone specimen, such as an *Echeveria agavoides* 'Ebony' at right, a specimen jade, or a crested succulent. Specimen plants such as these can still be the feature plant in a mixed bowl, providing they are large enough not to be drowned out or consumed by the other clustering or carpeting succulents. If you attend a succulent show, you will see a dish-garden display category, but most enthusiasts like to match their single specimen plant with a nice pot so you can really appreciate the intricacies of that particular plant.

Right: this is one of three almost identical low bowls on short pillars in front of a retail shop, nicely planted with varying colors and a front/back orientation. Designers have recently been going heavily into succulents for retail and commercial garden/hardscape plantscaping. Over the years I've seen pots like this filled with impatiens or vincas or any number of annuals that would look great for a time but need overhauls a few times a year. I always figured they would start to go more succulent, and that is happening now. Perhaps less work for the maintenance gardeners and bedding plant industry, but they are much more environmentally friendly and architecturaly pleasing. They still need an occasional but less frequent reworking, as even slow-growing succulents can become overgrown or get gangly over time.

Bottom right: a column-top low bowl of *Aeonium canariense* has reached their blooming potential simultaneously. What was a collection of low green disks are elongating into blooming cones, which will brown out and need replacing in a few months.

Below: a commercial installation of repeated egg-shaped planters have all been planted with crinkly echeverias and cascading 'red apple' ice plant, bringing low water lush beauty to a hardscape.

This office building brightened up its more stark and sterile feel with a series of succulent troughs. A combination of cascading and upright growers, with a mix of repeating colors, makes it a more inviting space.

Above and below right: A couple of well-done collections of fake, plastic succulents. These are best types of 'succulents' for low-light indoors.

You can create your own cascading succulent fountain by stacking progressively smaller pots on top of each other, and planting cascading succulents around the rims, with a combination of upright and cascading forms at the top. This creation is featured at the Madd Potter in Fallbrook, CA.

Left and above right: mixed succulent bowls by Courtyard Pottery.

Below right: a packed mixed succulent low bowl makes an excellent column topper.

As mentioned earlier, there are all kinds of ways to have fun with succulents. Almost any piece of furniture or equipment that can hold some soil, and hopefully allows drainage, can become a succulent garden. I can't think of a more dignified way for an old wheelbarrow, or especially an old toilet, to live out its final days.

SOFT SUCCULENTS IN THE LANDSCAPE

An echeveria-filled (looks like *E. elegans*, the aptly named 'Mexican Snowball') rock wall at Succulent Gardens nursery in Castroville, CA. Echeverias can grow this way in habitat.

I f you're planting an in-ground garden featuring soft succulents, or really pretty much any and all succulents, try to create a raised bed or mounding topography, using rocks and boulders. Plants look better in a non-flat, natural environment, and also will drain better during wet months. Most California topsoils are okay, unless you have thick adobe clay or very hard sandstone. The advantage to building mounds is that you don't have to dig down into the bad stuff – you can plant directly into the new, soft mounds you have created. Most rock and gravel yards will have an amended topsoil, which is usually good loamy native soil amended with something like mushroom compost, and perhaps some coarse sand or decomposed granite. This type of soil is fine, even though it might not be a 'cactus' mix. In fact, the cactus and succulent mixes aren't recommended for in-ground plantings, as the pumice and especially white perlite usually rise to the surface and looks messy. Be sure to plant in groupings and mass-plantings with at least some of your plants. Many of the soft succulents are small to medium in relative size, and won't be your feature plants, which might be aloes, agaves, cacti, etc.. Mass plantings of soft, understory or ground cover succulents will help you highlight your icon plants, and will also provide a colorful backdrop. In-ground succulent gardens need to be watered more frequently the first year or two to get your plants up to size, and you can slowly back off on the frequency as the garden matures.

The garden above left has somewhat of an ocean theme, featuring some succulents and other plants that mimic sea creatures or plants. The Asparagus meyeri blends well with the variegated *Kalanchoe fedschenkoi*, echeverias and senecios.

Above right: Succulent enthusiasts love mixing plants, but there's nothing wrong running with a mass planting of one favorite. The aeonium hybrid above lines a walkway in Santa Barbara.

Below: Purple *Senecio jacobsenii* and orange *Crassula capitella* 'Campfire' provide warm landscape color in this beachside garden in Cayucos, CA.

Above: whether in-ground as seen here or in containers, succulent combination is a fun and rewarding form of slow-motion art. At one time this was a dirt mound with some small, isolated plants a few feet apart, looking very man-made. But slowly the aeoniums, agave and cotyledons snuggled in together into the vignette seen here. If you could watch it unfold over time, the plants tend to blend and bleed together like a wet-on-wet watercolor painting, creating something you might have planned, but usually ends up different and even better than your original idea.

Most of the succulents in this book are viewed as container plants, due to necessity in non-mediterranean climates, but in California as well. They are just so cool and colorful and easy, happy in a pot, singly or in groups. But a number of them are major players in California landscapes, including most aeoniums, many crassulas (jades in particular), cotyledons, dudleyas, most kalanchoes – pretty much a large segment of all the groups highlighted on the following pages. Most don't reach the size of some of the larger succulents and cacti, but will serve as nice understory repetition plants, providing soft color swaths to compliment the iconic architectural plants.

Garden by
Solana Succulents
858 - 259 - 4563

Succulent plantings such as those seen here can have a sublime color pallet, not on the basis of flowers but from the plants themselves. In the example above, there is a rich green and burgundy theme, highlighted by the various aeoniums and red *Aloe cameronii*.

Right: soft succulents look great when planted in drifts that surround specimen plants or boulders.

On the previous pages you saw some exclusively 'soft succulent' landscapes, and of course they are beautiful. But consider blending them with at least a few of their more heavily armored relatives. I have owned a succulent nursery for many years and love all succulents, but I constantly run up against the (overly?) cautious parent, or grandparent, or dog/cat parent, that wants nothing to do with anything even remotely threatening. They may have had a bad encounter with a spine in their past, or associate the more spiny succulents with more of a 'desert' landscape. I've learned this is a battle I can't win. You want a 'girlie foo-foo' garden? I can do girlie foo-foo with just the plants in this book, and it will look great. But my standard response is to tell them that my kids and animals grew up around the spiky stuff, and they learned some valuable life lessons from daddy's plants.

Agaves, aloes, cacti and euphorbias and their ilk can provide wonderful, larger sculptural statements when situated among the softer plants. You can place them farther back where nobody should be able to get pricked unless they climbed back there to do it. And many of them, aloes and some euphorbias in particular, look more threatening than they really are. What appear to be spines are often very benign and you really have to grab hard and scrape to draw blood.

In the garden below, the dark *Aeonium zwartkop* provides a nice contrast with the the Golden Barrel cactus, and softens up the spikier agave and yucca in the background. Large boulders also offer a nice, natural framing device, and also some blank space to let your eye take a break from the botanical wonders. Don't let your plants grow so much that they cover the rocks over time.

Above: *Crassula* 'Blue Bird' and *Senecio barbertonicus*, both seen here in winter bloom, can create nice, pillowy mounds for a full and lush look.

At left, orange *Crassula* 'Campfire' contrasts nicely with *Echeveria* 'Afterglow'. Photo by Bob Wigand.

Below: Long-time California garden staples *Agave attenuata*, *Aeonium canariensis*, *Othonna capensis* and a procumbent form of rosemary provide a peaceful flow to the Del Mar Library garden. Design by Bill Teague.

Spinies and softies work together nicely in this Cardiff, CA. home. Built-in planting areas like these can be looked at as either landscape or large container garden situations, depending on your point of view. Sharper plants like aloes or agaves, such as *Agave americana* seen here, are usually larger specimens than the softer material. You can use the softer succulents both for color and accentuation as well as functionality, such as offering a visual border or buffer to stay away from the blue meanie in the middle.

At far left in the image at left is *Echium wilpretii*, which takes up some space but is an excellent succulent garden companion plant.

Below you see a few varieties of echeverias snuggled in with various non-succulent drought-tolerants, which can give a succulent garden a softer, natural look. But if you don't want to lose the smaller, slower-growing succulents, you'll need to trim the other plants back on occasion.

Often confused with natives are a whole host of non-succulent, compatible draught tolerant plants for mediterranean climates. Many of these are African or Australian natives, including sages, artemesias, proteas, leucospermums, certain grasses, flaxes, and all manner of other excellent landscape plants. Many of these plants are not great long-term in containers, or if they are they will sometimes overwhelm smaller succulents in the same pot. Likewise, many of the non-succulents are compatible in the landscape, but can grow much faster and overwhelm the generally smaller and slower growing succulents. Many can also grow woody and need replacing, so know what you are getting into before you plant that cute little 'Pride of Madeira' in the middle of your succulent garden.

Succulents, Natives, and Drought – Tolerants

A point made several times in this book is that probably 98% of the commercially available succulents are not from California or the southwest U.S. Most are from Africa, Mexico, Central/South America, the Canary Islands or Madagascar. Those of us in California are very lucky that so many of these foreigners love living here (sound familiar? I'm sure my Swedish grandparents thought so too). But is it more responsible to plant with natives than succulents? In my opinion it is a push, depending on what kind of plant material you like. I can appreciate a nice native garden, but I am obviously biased towards the exotic succulents, including those in this book and a whole host of other varieties. So, all things being equal, the only two issues regarding which is more environmentally responsible becomes water requirements and invasiveness.

Succulents are by definition low-water plants, but most do appreciate some dry season water to keep them looking nice. Many evolved in places that receive summer rainfall, which is rare in California. Most natives require very little or no off-season irrigation, with a trade-off that part of the natural cycle of native gardens is that they might not look as lush by the end of summer or early fall. Some nativists will dispute that, but that has been my observation. So a native garden likely will require slightly less water, but a succulent garden will come in a close second. And the longer a succulent garden abides, the less water they require. As mentioned earlier, you can pull off an absolute vacant-lot, no irrigation succulent garden with the right plants, but you won't have quite as many to choose from.

Regarding invasiveness, almost the only succulents that can escape their immediate area and possibly make it into natural areas via birds or wind are several of the 'ice plants', *Carpobrotus edulis* being the worst offender. *Mesembryanthemum crystallinum* and a few others have also invaded native areas, and have been sharing space in the wild for perhaps a hundred years. These belong on the 'do not plant' list, and indeed are almost impossible to find for sale at nurseries anymore. Other succulents that will reproduce unassisted, such as 'Mother of Millions' kalanchoes that drop offsets, or jades that will reproduce when pieces fall off and root, tend to stay in the immediate shadow of the parent plant, and will not populate a large enough area to be any threat to native plants.

One of the best parts of my job as a nursery owner has been my buying trips to wholesale and backyard growers. Even though I rarely take home plants anymore (after 25 years of owning the nursery, the yard is full. Sad emoji). It is fun to find something new or unusual growing among the more common 'bread and butter' succulents. Every grower has an 'off-limits' greenhouse dedicated to propagation stock and various treasures they can't part with. The photo above right was from the late Dick Bogart's off-limits house near Ojai, CA. Dick was one of the greats and a true plantsman. Above left is part of the sprawling operation of Succulent Gardens in Watsonville, CA. Much of Succulent Gardens is retail, and well worth a visit. At left is just one of hundreds of production greenhouses of a large wholesale grower in Vista, CA. The inventory is mind-boggling.

Where they come from

Most of the succulents in this book have roots in Africa, Mexico, the Canary Islands, and other faraway lands, but by now can claim to be multi-generational Californians. Most succulents available today are grown by medium and large professional growers, many located in Southern California. Since most are so easy to propagate and succulents in general have become so popular of late, many growers are either switching over from bedding plants to succulents, or at least devoting a larger segment of their production to them. There are quite a few backyard growers that make at least a supplemental income by devoting a few tables in their backyard to succulent propagation, some going so far as to build a small greenhouse. A greenhouse isn't necessary in coastal California, but it can provide a bit of an artificially warm and humid atmosphere that can get seedlings or cuttings established, as well as protection from cold wintertime temperatures or storm events.

Large and small growers are both involved in creating new hybrids or isolating and propagating unique cultivars. New species from habitat still finds their way to market as well, typically collected legally by botanical gardens or foundations, eventually to be released to larger growers for further propagation and introduction. The Huntington Botanical Gardens releases new material – hybrids, cultivars, or new species material – annually via its International Succulent Introductions (ISI) venture.

A grower's offering of the coveted *Echeveria cante*, happily basking in the full sun of Fallbrook, California.

We plant geeks, uh, enthusiasts, are lucky to be living in somewhat of a golden age of new and abundant availability. That applies to ornamental plants as a whole, but I can tell you from experience that there are just so many new and wonderful succulents available today. I would estimate that well over half of the species, cultivars or hybrids that I have at my nursery were either unavailable or yet to be created when I opened in the early nineties. Although many of the larger plant species have been discovered in the wild and introduced over the past hundred years, there are still new species being identified and brought into cultivation via botanical garden introductions. An even greater number of hybrids and cultivars are being developed. I've been in the business for almost thirty years, and I still keep finding something new when I visit growers or collectors, which typically will take a slow journey from collector plant to wider introduction.

Care and Feeding
Soil, Water, Light, etc . . .

All the images in this book were taken in California. I've lived my whole life in California. All my knowledge about these plants is based on how I've known them to grow here, and for those of you not in mediterranean climates, I apologize. We're spoiled. For us out west, these are the idiot-proof plants. Lots of sun, don't let them freeze or stay wet too long, and all is good. So the cultural tips and advice I impart in this book are based on what I know about how they live in our climate.

I know customers from back east that visit my nursery that are just nuts about succulents, and have their greenhouses and techniques to baby them through the winters. You guys gotta do what you gotta do, and I admire you for it.

Having said that, with the exception of the dudleyas, none of these plants are California natives. Most come from parts of Mexico, Africa, Madagascar, or the Canary Islands, the latter of which is the closest match to our California coastal climate. We do have climate-related issues here as well, which I'll discuss below.

California has a number of climates or climate zones. A huge swath of our population inhabits the areas where we have the least amount of environmental stress – from the coast to the foothills, San Diego to San Francisco. The farther north you go, the wetter the winters can be, and some plants are fine with that – aeoniums in particular. The farther east you go, you begin to encounter summer heat and eventually desert or mountain conditions, which many of these plants will have difficulty with. I'll tell you all I know about each group of plants discussed in this book, and when I venture to advise for ranges out of my coastal zone, the advice will be anecdotal but hopefully correct.

For the most part, all of these succulents like sun. The farther inland you go, and the more you approach triple digit summer heat, many or most would prefer partial shade, but still need as much sun as they can take to maintain color. California typically experiences warm, dry summers and cool and (hopefully) wet winters. Most succulents are fine with this, particularly winter growers like aeoniums. A majority do experience significant summer rains where they are from, so despite being 'low water' plants, they will be quite happy with once-a-week summer water. The rare summer rainfall we receive is a blessing for almost all of these plants.

No environment is exactly like a similar climate from another part of the globe. Even comparing mediterranean climates, ours is unique for several reasons. Our dry Santa Ana wind events can be quite stressful to all kinds of creatures. Our winter rains can come in quite heavy at times, compared to more gentle drizzle rains of other locales. And in particular, I think California can experience more significant weather extremes in a short time period, enough to occasionally burn a plant that might otherwise accept the heat-up if built more slowly. I've seen some desert-tolerant agaves get burned on the coast, shortly after a winter rain condition turned rapidly into a dry, hot Santa Ana. But we still have it pretty good here, and I probably should stop whining about our 'hardships' in California. I can feel the sarcastic 'boo hoos' from New York and Ohio as I write this.

If you're growing soft succulents in pots, you should use a 'cactus' or 'cactus and succulent' soil, which should be a light, fast-draining mix, with a combination of organics and light material such as perlite or pumice. Succulents like to get wet, and then dry out in between waterings. A good watering schedule is once a week, more in times of high temperatures, and less in cool or rainy weather. In a typical California winter, assuming we return to those regularly someday, I don't water much from November through March, unless there is a lengthy stretch of warm, dry weather. In the non-rainy season, try to water once a week, but most established succulents will survive a few weeks without water.

Fertilizing can be important, much more so for plants in containers than in the ground. Potted plants can deplete the nutrients in the soil after a while, which makes feeding more important. There are lots of theories about what to feed and how much. I have always been a minimalist on babying my plants, which to me is a part of the appeal of succulents. They are okay with lazy owners. Fish emulsion fertilizer is good, or almost any plant food you might own, but whatever the recommended dosage is, dilute it by at least half. Too much fertilizer is a bit like bulking them up on steroids, which in the long run isn't good for them. Benign semi-neglect is acceptable. I don't feed every watering – but more like when I feel like making the extra effort, or if it looks like some of the plants are stressed.

To correct for California's alkaline water, a simple formula to increase the acidity (sounds bad, but is actually good) is to add a tablespoon of distilled white vinegar per 5 gallons of tap water. This is not the same as fertilizer, but should increse the acidity to a better level which will let the plant absorb nutrients more efficiently. You can also add your properly diluted fertilizer to the same 5 gallons. You don't need to do this every watering, and I usually water my collection with overhead watering from the hose with a rain nozzle without that extra step, which I only do occasionally for some of the more prized plants. And be sure to get them out into the rain when possible. Nothing beats rain water. Just ask the weeds.

Aeonium 'Mardis Gras'

Some nurseries will include care instructions for their succulents that advise against too much sun. I dispute this, at least in the coastal zone. Sometimes a plant that came directly from a greenhouse or shady store might burn when first placed in the sun, but most will acclimate when the new growth begins. For the most part, these are sun-loving plants from subtropical to desert climates, and the sun will bring out the color. Juvenile plants might need more protection, but older plants should get as much sun as they can tolerate. The farther inland you live, the more shade some might need, but try to get them at least some of the more forgiving morning sun, or filtered light.

Plants generally prefer to live outdoors in the elements, but will live indoors if close enough to a window to get strong, preferably direct sunlight for at least a few hours a day. There are a few exceptions of succulents that are more shade tolerant, such as haworthias and Christmas Cactus, but for the most part, don't think of these as houseplants. They will prefer your sunny patio.

Since I've owned a succulent nursery for quite a while, I am often in early on new introductions. When Altman Plants introduced the variegated *Aeonium* 'Mardis Gras' a while back, I made sure to buy one (only one; they were and still are sort of expensive). I took it home and placed it into my scientifically rigorous testing program, wherein I stick it in a pot with the rest of my collection of strange and neglected wierdlings and pretty much forget about it. I try to water once a week in the non-rainy season, but I'm not consistent about that. My plants at home don't get as much attention as the plants at my nursery – I'm sort of like the mechanic that doesn't want to work on his own car or the plumber that needs to fix his own leaky pipes.

The second image is the same 'Mardis Gras' that I bought two years prior as a single, maybe 4" plant. It looks okay here, but not quite as fine as the greenhouse-happy plant photographed by John Trager on page 90. It has a reputation as being somewhat of a difficult grower compared to some of its relatives, and I can attest to that. This particular plant was given up for dead – or at least it appeared to be heavily leaning that way – a few times. Like most aeoniums, it tended to contract in summer heat, and almost collapsed at one point. I moved it into a shadier place and forgot about it, but after a very wet winter, I was surprised to see it had multiplied and was looking relatively good. Then a few months later into the spring, it began transitioning into an almost completely dark, plum colored phase, left. I guess it pays tribute to its different parentage depending on conditions and time of year.

A few years after its introduction, I have yet to see any large and vigorous clumps of this plant in the landscape, but perhaps in time it will adjust and become as much of a staple as *A*. 'Sunburst' or *A*. 'Kiwi'. For now it is still more of a collector plant, best kept in containers. This is how it goes with succulents, and plants in general. They have to adjust the level of benign neglect that most of us subject them to, and they either adapt as low-maintenance plants, or remain in the province of collectors that know how and when to baby them.

Don't think of soft succulents as indoor plants. They love sun, at least up to a point. If you want to enjoy them indoors, or have to due to your climate, they should occupy the sunniest window you have – preferably at least a few hours of direct sun through the glass per day. The farther from the window you get, the more they will etiolate and stretch, and slowly lose their color. They may adapt to bright indirect light, but will look better with some sun. If they have been in a lower light situation for a long time and you want to let them recharge their solar batteries, you should slowly phase them in to being outside in the sun, as they need time to adjust to the higher light. Sometimes they will burn in the sun if they don't have time to adjust – so don't assume that they prefer low light or shade. As pointed out on page 24, they are making some fantastic fake plastic succulents, which are the best types for your darker interiors.

So much color and nary a flower in sight. That is a huge part of the attraction of the soft succulents – permanent, if sometimes seasonally shifting, color!

Right:
Aeonium 'Kiwi' in late spring peak hot coloration.

Below: soft, pillowy drifts of *Crassula undulata*, Golden Jade, Silver Dollar Jade and *Aeonium Zwartkop* play together nicely at Waterwise Botanicals in Bonsall, CA.

Below: an unidentified echeveria hybrid, possible 'Andromeda' in tight lavender-pastel crinkly globes.

Succulents can have some remarkable built-in survival systems. In the image above left, an aeonium suffered from a heat spell without enough water and its stems withered along the central trunk. I had trouble figuring out whether to use this image in the 'propagation' section or the 'what can go wrong' section, as it applies to both. Once the rosettes realized they were cut off, they began to send out new roots, anticipating eventually falling off and hopefully connecting with the ground and growing. In this case I gave them a hand, since I was the negligent owner. The new family is doing well. Middle and right, a *cristate echeveria* with a section that had detached, fallen, and got caught up on the way down, allowing it to callous off and new roots to form, seen in close up at right. It doesn't get much easier to start a new plant when they just do it themselves. Plants courtesy of Tina Zucker.

Sometimes the plants do all the work on their own via seed – as nature intended. However, even though many non-native succulents thrive in California, few will actually grow from seed unassisted. That is likely due to our summer-dry season not corresponding to wet and warm seasons in their native habitats. Dudleyas, however, are local and seedlings often will sprout at the foot of the mother plant. The collection of little ones in the photo below left popped up at my house, below the parent *D. brittoni* planted on a north-facing rockery. I love when that happens (that sentiment does not apply to the 'Mother of Millions' kalanchoes, see page 255).

Right: an example of a new cluster of rosettes growing out from the point of decapitation. The detached main head (at left) will root as well. This appears to be *Aeonium* 'Mardis Gras', which is a patented plant, so I may have unwittingly photographed a crime. I'll never roll over though.

Propagation

Most of the succulent plants in this book are easy to propagate – some ridiculously so. Most can be started via cuttings, some will form new plants simply from a detached leaf, others form ready-to-go plantlets along the leaf, and some (dudleyas) usually have to be started from seed, which can be a fun and rewarding challenge but not exactly easy. Plants that form stems can usually be propagated by detaching some stem with new growth at the tip. Just let the severed piece dry for a few days, plant it in a cactus/succulent mix, and treat it like a plant, and after a few weeks it should have roots and begin to grow. This works well with most aeoniums and many crassulas, such as the jades.

Some echeverias, graptopetalums, pachyphytums and kalanchoes will grow new plantlets at the base of a severed leaf, as the grower is working on above left. In this case, just leave the leaf exposed and a new plant, and roots, will form at the base of the dying leaf. The 'mother of millions' kalanchoes are the easiest of all – you will find baby plants growing in the pot where they landed with no help from you at all.

Many succulents, including most echeverias and their kin, will form offsets or 'pups' that will emerge under the parent plant, and can easily be wiggled off, often with roots ready to go. Even if you don't get any roots, as long as you have a rosette and stem, it likely will form roots. Just plant and wait.

A few genera in this book, including most dudleyas and some mesembs, will have to be seed-started. Seed collection can be a challenge, assuming fertile seed is available, and can be as fine as dust. There are many theories of propagating via seed, and I'm not going to offer them all here, but I do encourage you to give it a try. My experience is that it isn't that hard to get seed to germinate, but coaxing little seedlings through the first months can be very difficult, due to 'damping off', wherein moss or fungus can take over your damp environment. I generally leave seed starting to the professionals. If a plant seems expensive for its size, it might be because it had to be started from seed, and has taken three years to reach a 6-inch pot size.

Above middle: some or the more rare echeverias are reluctant to form offsets, such as *E. cante* seen here. One way to create more, if you're up to the challenge of mutilating a prized plant, is to detach the growing meristem, saving just enough of the rosette for it to grow new roots and keep living. If you leave a ring of leaves on the rest of the now-decapitated plant, it will hopefully generate several new heads clustered around the stem, which can be detached and started individually. Inset: a severed echeveria head newly rooted in a perlite medium.

Above left: this was a nice carpet of clustering *Echeveria harmsii*, but after a while it became gangly and woody, struggling to survive. It may have experienced too long of a spell without water, or perhaps the soil just proved to be too nutrient poor. It won't come back from being this far gone, so it should be removed and replaced with something more durable. Above right: *Sedum* 'Burrito', or 'Donkey Tail', is a rather fragile plant, and either the elements or birds can cause empty stem portions, as seen here. The plant is still healthy, it just looks a little beat up. Still kind of cool.

Below left: A few years ago I noticed all my *Aeonium* 'Sunburst' developed black or brown marks. And everybody else's did too, which tells me it was due to environmental stress, in this case a sudden spring heat spell, that obviously affected a variegated plant such as this more than its green cousins. Notice how after several months this plant has pushed out clean new growth from the center. The old leaves will eventually fall and you'll have your pretty and perfect plant back – at least until the next hot spell. Below right shows an *Aeonium canariense* that was on the menu for some nibbler, likely a snail or slug. This happens, usually in wet winters. You can kill the snails by any means your conscience allows. I like a 9-iron.

Things that can go wrong with 'easy' plants

As a general rule, most of the plants in this book are mediterranean types, and don't take well to a freeze or too much triple digit heat. In winter months, many can handle a cold, dry night where temperatures approach but don't quite reach freezing, but the kiss of death is often the combination of wet and cold. As much as succulents enjoy rain water, if you have potted plants still wet from a rain, with clear and cold nights approaching, I'd recommend getting them out of the elements, at least until they dry out. I have a handful of my more sensitive plants living outdoors through the winter, but keep them under a fiberglass awning without heat, which will at least let them stay dry to survive the cold.

Heat is another issue. Aeoniums are coastal and are almost impossible in desert conditions. Many other succulents also recoil from desert summer heat, but can survive if kept under shade cloth or given filtered or morning-only sun. Sometimes the heat itself isn't the problem, but rather the intensity of the sun, which can also overheat the containers the plants may be in. Another sun concern we sometimes have in California occurs during fall or spring, when Santa Ana events, combined with a lower-angle sun, can burn stems or trunks that are from more equatorial climates that may be very hot, but have a more diffused and overhead sun angle.

Another occasional incident we may experience are extreme weather swings, from wet winter conditions to hot and dry Sana Anas within a day or two. It can be too much of an adjustment for a plant's tissue that evolved in a place where such conditions may never occur.

Above: This aeonium didn't react well to a few frosty nights in Walnut Creek, CA. Other succulents in the area were okay, but aeoniums in particular are frost averse.

Below is an echeveria that suffered from too much wetness. The lower leaves in contact with wet winter soil couldn't dry out and molded away. If you clean away the affected leaves, the plant should rebound if the rosette is still good. .

Bottom image is another echeveria that has developed an ugly skin condition as a result of environmental stress (possibly exacerbated by a viral infection) again likely due to too much winter cold and wet. Such damage won't go away, but eventually new leaves will replace the old as they fall off. For some reason I mostly see this phenomenon on the thick-skinned, carunculated *E. gibbiflora* hybrids.

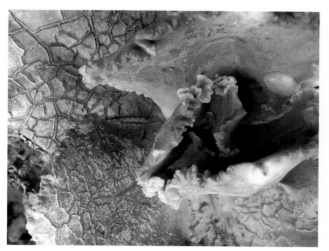

If it makes you feel any better, sometimes plants just die and you'll never know why, but you shouldn't consider it your fault. I've owned a succulent nursery for many years and have killed tons of plants. Some I'll take responsibility for due to negligence (although that is usually something succulents are okay with). But in other cases, I've had flats of the same plants, same genetic stock, same soil, same light and water, and absent any visible signs of bugs, one or two will just give up the ghost. I suppose you could do some serious botanical forensics to find the cause if you really wanted to, but I prefer to use the 'stuff happens' excuse and move on. Throw the dead guy away as soon as you can – out of sight, out of mind.

Order: Saxifragales
Family: Crassulaceae
Genus: Aeonium
Species: canariense

AEONIUMS

Aeonium canariense

Aeoniums are rosette succulents, similar at first blush to echeverias. The primary difference is that aeoniums are more thin-leaved, with barely visible 'teeth' on the leaf edges, and are more prone to grow vertically on stems. They also are more prolific at clustering into large clumps, easy to divide. They experience a greater period of expansion and contraction, depending on the season. Another difference is that aeoniums are monocarpic (once-and-done) bloomers, wherin an individual rosette becomes the flower. This will be illustrated a bit further on.

Aeoniums (usually pronounced 'ay-OH-nee-um', occasionally 'eye-OH-nee-um') are primarily from the Canary Islands, which have a mediterranean, coastal, summer-dry/winter-wet climate that is very similar to coastal California, so most of

these beautiful rosette-on-stem plants grow great in that environment. While I wouldn't consider them invasive, there are some old established colonies occupying abandoned lots and cliff sides all over coastal California. My friends in the local deserts and Arizona can have a difficult time with many of the soft succulents, but aeoniums in particular give them fits when exposed to desert heat. They just prefer to be near the beach, or at least west of the coastal foothills. I have that issue as well.

While the majority of species are endemic to the Canaries as well as the Cape Verde Islands and Madeira, there are small populations on the west coast of Africa, and surprisingly, several are from East Africa. The likely explanation is that at one time they ranged all the way across northern and central Africa, but then the Sahara Desert happened, and the remnant populations east of the desert that lived in climates wet enough to support them survived.

Aeoniums are winter growers, and will tolerate but don't require much dry-season watering. They are used to curling up and conserving water through the dry summer months. They are fantastic in the landscape or in containers, provided you live within the parameters discussed above.

As you'll see on the following pages, we have a number of true species in captivity in the U.S., but there are a greater number of hybrids, some intentional, others probably not. If you can locate the now out-of-print book at right, *Aeonium in Habitat and Cultivation* by Rudolf Shulz, you will own what I consider to be one of the best

This book gets my vote for the best succulent book devoted to a particular genus, or maybe just best succulent book, period.

A colony of happy aeoniums at Succulent Gardens in Watsonville, CA.

Above: an unidentified blushing hybrid, likely a Catlin hybrid such as A. 'Cyclops', in happy winter glory at the San Luis Obispo Botanic Garden.

succulent books ever made. The photography is outstanding, with great habitat images, and the information is as thorough as you could hope for. I can't be as thorough in this book, but if you decide you really like this genus, you'll love his book.

A related and more obscure genus is aichryson, comprised of mostly smaller, clustering plants from the same habitat. Some aeoniums are occasionally lumped in with that genus, and vice versa.

Some aeoniums can and will change color. The same flat of 4-inch plants to right were photographed a few weeks apart. Just a few weeks prior to the image taken middle right, all the plants in the flat were green with a little red lipstick edging, similar to the few still-green plants on the right part of the image. But some of the plants were beginning to turn burgundy-purple at that time, perhaps due to the increasing springtime sun angle. Just two weeks later, the entire flat of plants had colored up (bottom right), which should last through the summer before turning green again in the fall. The plants were never identified by the grower, but I'd venture a guess that it might be the cross called 'Plum Purdy', based on the plum coloration. You can see an example of this same phenomenon with *Aeonium* 'Mardis Gras' on page 42.

Above: three varieties of *aeonium* are melded into one mound in Los Osos, CA. The blooming portion at left is *Aeonium arboreum*, the small-rosette large cluster in the middle appears to be *Aeonium haworthii*,and the large individual at the bottom is *Aeonium canariense*.

While researching and photographing aeoniums for this book, I became an even greater fan of the genus. Part of that is gaining more of an appreciation of the diversity of the group, the complexity of all the hybrids, and particularly by appreciating how happy they are living in coastal California.

Below: like many succulents, aeoniums will sometimes spontaneously form a crest, providing a slice of unexpected psychedelic coolness in an already cool plant.

Of all the imported succulents that have gained a toehold in the Golden State, aeoniums have best assimilated and have effortlessly become true locals, like they've been here all along.

Top left: some of the long-established California *aeoniums*, which in fact may be hybrids, are the green vertical-growing *Aeonium arboreum*, shown blooming at top, and the larger, lower growing *Aeonium canariense* (hybrid?) below. With just an occasional spritz of dry-season watering, these aeoniums can provide year-round green in coastal climates.

Top Right: there are various black forms of *Aeonium atropurpureum*, the darkest of which is known as *v. Zwartkop*', seen here. It can be a stunning contrast plant in any garden.

Above: a partially variegated example of *Aeonium* 'Sunburst'.

Above: aeoniums love a rainy day. They are also among the best succulents for semi-shady and wetter parts of your yard. This is particularly true for many of the green aeoniums, either species or hybrids. If you're slowly trying to work a few succulents into your more traditional flower garden, these might be good 'gateway' succulents as soft, green compliment plants. Once you get tired of replanting all your annual bedding plants, you can use the aeoniums as a foundation to build your new lower-water succulent garden around. And if you thin out or remove the shade-casting trees, the aeoniums are absolutely fine in full sun as well – at least within the coastal and inland valley realms.

Right: seasonal red leaf edges will appear, usually in the late winter to spring months.

Above, a majority of this cluster is going into full spring bloom. It will look really cool and interesting for a few months, but then sort of ugly and brown and full of holes for a while. The next fall rains should bring it back via new growth below the expired stalks.

Left: aeoniums can be considered 'monocarpic' bloomers, meaning that at a certain point of maturity, the entire rosette will morph into a large flower cone, which will eventually turn brown and crispy as it dies. However, most aeoniums are clumpers, so even if one or several rosettes bloom themselves out, there usually are more rosettes waiting to take their place. In the case at left, a large *Aeonium canariense* in the later stages of flower, resembling descending fireworks.

Below: there is, or was, an aeonium under all those flowers. This *Aeonium davidbramwellii* (?) bloomed itself out of existence. There were five or six heads, but they all decided to bloom at the same time.

At my nursery I've noticed some folks are attracted to aeoniums, but are reluctant to plant them as they have a reputation for getting 'lanky' or 'weedy' over time. While this can be true, quite often, either with or without help, they can eventually regenerate new, lower growth to replace the bloomed out parts. And I would argue that aeoniums are just like so many non-succulent plants, requiring an occasional pruning back, just a bit more than most succulents. And they almost always will look better in the winter and spring months, so just wait it out and they will come back nicely.

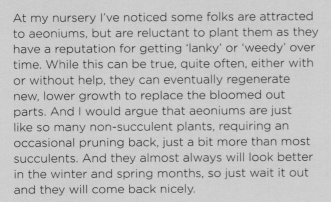

Above: an old stand of *Aeonium atropurpureum* in mid-spring.

Above: this is how an aeonium reacts to hot and dry times. It can contract into an almost closed rosette to conserve water and reduce sun exposure. Below: this is a typical phase of older aeoniums: long stems, small contracted heads. A rainy winter will cause the plants to flush out somewhat, but really old clumps sometimes never quite make it back to their old floraceous glory days.

Middle right is a naturalized colony of *Aeonium arboreum*. It is clinging to a cliff close to the beach in Southern California. Above it is a band of native vegetation, and a piece of planted aeonium from the yard above likely tumbled down through the natives, found a toe-hold on the slope, and found itself a home very similar to vertical bluffs it grows on in its native Canary Island habitat. The bottom right image shows more of the same colony that has tumbled all the way down to the street below, where another population has formed. I don't consider aeoniums to be invasive in California, as it rarely if ever broadcasts itself unassisted by seed, but it can stake a claim to a small area via vegetatively moving itself around.

Background photo: a characteristic of most aeoniums is relatively thin leaves with small, fine 'hairs' along the leaf edges, as seen in this example of *A. tabuliforme*.

In the Canary Islands, aeoniums occupy a similar niche to that of the dudleyas in California. They love to find a toehold in a rocky outcropping and live vertically. Top left: *Aeonium calderense*. Top right: *Aeonium decorum*. Middle left: *Aeonium nobile*. Middle right: *Aeonium davidbramwellii*. Left: *Aeonium lindleyi*. Right: *Aeonium palmense* in bloom.

Left: the small-leaved *A. lindleyi* is famous for being the 'antidote plant' for euphorbia sap. I haven't had the opportunity to use it myself yet (like most people, the sap only hurts when it gets in the eyes), but it is good to have around just in case.

Aeoniums in Habitat

I have yet to visit the Canary Islands, but Nels Christensen is working off his bucket list and provided me these images from his travels there. As mentioned earlier, there are quite a few aeoniums that are still not common in California cultivation, including a few on these pages. For example, the aeoniums below, *A. subplanum*, and *A. cunneatum*, bottom, are very familiar looking plants, but are rarely identified as such in nurseries. There is a good chance that many of our unidentified 'garden' aeoniums are in fact species such as these, or more likely hybrids of them.

At left is *Aeonium urbicum* with a heck of an ocean view. Note the non-native immigrant opuntia cactus.

All images on this spread by Nels Christensen.

The image at left shows *A. arboreum* in an early stage of rosette contraction in late spring. They will also occasionally acquire a red/pink blush during this period, shown above. Prior to the first fall rains, these rosettes will be tight little fists about half this size. After significant winter rains, it will flush back out to a bush so full, the stems won't even be visible.

Below is an example of *A. arboreum 'holochrysum'*, a subspecies that exhibits remarkable tanic stripes, most pronounced in fall and winter. By summer the stripes almost disappear, and from a distance the shrunken heads will appear a dull greenish brown.

Aeonium arboreum

Aeonium arboreum is probably one of the first and foremost aeoniums to have escaped from the Canary Islands several hundred years ago. Colonies have been growing unassisted in the same California yards, occupied or abandoned, since at least the turn of the last century. It has just about become a native plant (see the examples on page 57). It loves winter and survies long hot summers, with showy yellow flowers in winter and spring. There is a variegated form, shown below left and middle, sometimes called 'luteovariegatum' that isn't quite as durable as the larger variegated plant, *Aeonium* 'Sunburst' (pg. 87). The row below left, however, has found a happy place along this Leucadia, CA driveway. Bottom right: this species has perhaps the showiest bright yellow flower cones of the genus.

Aeonium canariense, seen here sharing space with an *Aeonium* Catlin hybrid, is a great low-effort succulent to occupy large areas, in either full-sun or fairly shady portions of the garden.

Below left: the rose-tinged outer leaves on both the foreground and background aeonium clumps are typical of late spring, as outer leaves begin to die off. The plant in front is a typically large *A. canariense*, the out-of-focus background plant is likely a Jack Catlin hybrid. Below right is a happy cluster in early spring bloom. *Aeonium canariense* has a large creamy white-yellow flower in contrast to the bright yellow bloom of *A. arboreum*.

Aeonium canariense

The default name of this big garden staple is *Aeonium canariense*, but I have also seen it called *A. urbicum*, and is perhaps a hybrid of either or both. It is also referred to as the 'dinner plate' (the rosette is certainly that big), but occasionally that epithet seems to belong to *A. tabuliforme* (pg. 84), which would also make sense. At any rate, this large and robust plant will occupy a relatively sizable portion of your garden if you let it. It is very durable, and will follow the seasonal expansion/contraction of most aeoniums. It can take a while to bloom out, but as you can see from the image on page 56, it can have a spectacular and large flowering

event. The flower tends to be more of a vanilla cream color than the brighter yellow of some of the other species aeoniums. This is one of more predominant aeoniums in the California landscape, and it can get huge after winter rains, with rosettes over two feet across.

There is a tight mound of clumpy, green aeonium in my neighborhood, only the rosettes of this rarely-watered sidewalk-adjacent pant were too small and compact to be *A. canariense*. Then after a particularly wet winter, it turned into precisely this plant. Aeoniums are like that.

Aeonium hierrense

Also known as the Giant Houseleek, this big aeonium is usually a single-head plant with a trunk that resembles a palm or cycad, almost like you'd draw up an imaginary, kind of comical succulent plant. It is monocarpic like most aeoniums, blooming out with pink flowers at 3 to 5 years. It is easy to grow but hard to find, as it must be seed-started. If you like aeoniums, this should be on your list. Until researching this book, I had rarely encountered this plant, but it has become one of my favorites. This beauty is reaching maturity at Los Osos Valley Nursery near Morro Bay.

A closely related, similar looking and recently described species is *Aeonium escobarii*.

Aeonium undulatum

This is one of the largest and best of the aeoniums, with vibrant and shiny green, undulating leaves on stems that can reach chest to head high. It seems to be more prevalent in Central and Northern California, perhaps preferring the slightly cooler and wetter conditions. The happy plant above lives in Oakland, CA. It is distinguishable from *Aeonium urbicum* (following page) by its glossy and wavy leaves, but grows similarly large rosettes on tall stems.

Aeonium urbicum

Aeonium urbicum and *A. ciliatum* are pretty much indistinguishable from what I've been able to tell. Both are generally tall-growing, single-rosette plants that will occasionally offset close to the base. Apparently they are difficult to distinguish in habitat as well, and will hybridize. *A. ciliatum* should have a rough stem, leaving a pattern of leaf scars. *A. urbicum* a smoother stem, which looks to be much thicker and stouter in habitat photos as opposed to the California plants seen here. The plants at left I believe are *A. urbicum*. The one below was identified by the Huntington Botanical Garden as *A. ciliatum*. Below left at Lotus Land in Santa Barbara would appear to be *A. ciliatum* as well. True species of both should have pinkish flowers.

Aeonium ciliatum

Photo: John Traeger

Aeonium percarneum

(x. *ciliatum* or x *A. davidbramwellii?*)

This long-leaved aeonium, which comes in a few iterations, has given me fits with identification. I showed images to a few experts, and the typical response was along the lines of 'Oh yeah, that one', with a few species names offered, which leads me to believe that it is an old hybrid that may be comprised of *A. percarneum* with *A. ciliatum* or *A. urbicum*, and/or *A. davidbramwellii*, or maybe something else entirely. I can't find anything like it in Schulz' book, with the excpetion of an image of *A. davidbramwellii* with exceptionally long leaves due to growing in the shade. But the plants here are in full sun. It does have a long-leaved habit, similar to *A.* 'Sunburst', which is also not a positively identified plant. It can be a single- or multiple-head plant, which the true species listed in the heading usually aren't.

Below: This big green flower of a plant looks like whatever the cross or cultivar that Aeonium 'Sunburst' sported from (most likely *A. davidbramwellii* is involved). The shape is almost identical to that plant, but appears to either have reverted from the variegated form, or perhaps has existed all along as the less glamorous green sibling.

Earlier in this chapter I talked about the fantastic book *Aeonium in Habitat and Cultivation* by Australian nurseryman Rudolf Schulz. Based on his work and experience, I consider him to be about as close to an expert on the genus as there is. Following is his book preface, which I think accurately sums up the difficulty in identifying so many aeoniums, outside of a handful of easily identifiable species and hybrids.

"My first trip to the Canary Islands was arranged when I became increasingly annoyed by not knowing what aeonium I was looking at in cultivation. As a nurseryman, I am supposed to know my plants, but when I had to decline a firm identification just about every time I was asked for one, I decided to visit the main habitats and sort the genus out for myself.

The plants in habitat were not only beautiful, they were also relatively consistent. Hybrids were found, but not as many or in such large stands that identification became difficult. I went home with a false sense of confidence, feeling that I knew all the Canary Island species well enough to make a firm identification. When confronted with the twenty-five or so aeoniums available in cultivation, it was irritating to find identification was still almost impossible. Were these plants hybrids? Were they cultivars that were atypical for the species? Were their diagnostic characteristics masked by growing in cultivation without the normal stresses of habitat? The answer is most certainly yes to all three possibilities. So I needed to go back for further research. While still often confused, aeonium-wise, I now at least have an idea why I am confused! Hopefully this book will help the collector sort out some of the mystery of aeoniums. Fortunately for the gardener, identification is less of an issue than for the collector, and this book will provide insights and inspiration for gardeners interested in aeoniums."

Rudolf Schulz, June 4, 2007

Aeonium . . . green hybrids

There are all manner of green, clumping aeoniums in cultivation, and I'm convinced that most are un-named hybrids. Distinct from the more upright, stem-forming *A. arboreum* (which still might be a contributor), most of these plants are likely some cross of either *A. balsamiferum, A. canariense, A. castello-paivae, A. cuneatum, A. decorum, A. haworthii, A. undulatum* or *A. spathulatrum*. Very few of these distinct species are sold as such in the plant trade, and even botanic gardens feature some of these excellent mounding plants without identification. An exception is *A. haworthii*, which is basically the non-variegated form of A. 'Kiwi', with an identical rosette, but it tends to grow into a larger bush (see page 95). There are some named hybrids, such as 'Emerald Carpet' or 'Shamrock' but proper identification of plants that look like those seen here can be almost impossible. Just enjoy them.

This is a variable plant, probably due to hybridization in cultivation, distinguished by dark red to purple leaf color, usually with a degree of green, especially on the inside of the rosettes. It differs from the much more uniformly black or purple (depending on how you interpret color) of *A. atropurpureum* 'Zwartkop' (page 73) in generally being a much fuller plant with a multitude of smaller heads, nor does it grow quite as tall.

Aeonium atropurpureum

Not a true species, this plant is technically identified as *Aeonium arboreum v. atropurpureum*. It is essentially a form or cultivar of *A. arboreum* that displays various degrees of red/black outer leaf coloration. It can be an unstable trait, and occasionally you will see a portion of a cluster reverting to the pure green form. To complicate matters, there are a few named and un-named hybrids and cultivars with varying growth habits and coloring characteristics. But they're all nice.

Plants can get confused sometimes. Aeoniums typically flower in a cone fashion as seen on the facing page, wherein the entire rosette morphs into the bloom. In this case, an *Aeonium zwartkop* has opted for a halo effect flower.

Aeonium 'Zwartkop'

The classic form of A. 'Zwartkop' in full bloom.

Properly known as *Aeonium arboreum* 'Zwartkop' (but most of us don't bother with the middle name), this is one of the most striking of the aeoniums, particularly to folks that have never seen a 'black' plant before (I see black; some folks see purple or even describe it as red!). It is also known as the 'Black Rose', or the 'Holland Clone', as the original sport that exhibited this characteristic was identified and isolated in Holland many years ago. The name means 'black head' in Dutch, but is often called 'Schwartzkopf', which means the same thing in German. It tends to have larger heads on taller stocks than the plant it is derived from, and the extra dark foliage is quite striking, especially when contrasted with the bright yellow flower cone. It is stable, as I've never seen one to revert to the green form as cv. *atropurpureum* can do. It seems to be a little more prone than most aeoniums to becoming small heads on tall stocks with age, and you might need to replace them after 5 to 10 years if that look begins to grow tiresome.

A crested example of A. 'Zwartkop'

Catlin hybrids

Jack Catlin was a well known hybridizer and volunteer horticulturalist at the Huntington Garden in Los Angeles. He worked with the dark 'Zwartkop' to make many crosses, some quite successful, and a few at times hard to identify. The plants featured on these pages are likely all Catlin hybrids, with names such as *Aeonium* 'Velour', 'Plum Purdy', 'Blushing Beauty', and the eponymous 'Jack Catlin'. All of the aforementioned are generally tight, mounding, low clumpers as seen here. Two of his larger/taller crosses are A. 'Voodoo' and 'Cyclops', featured on the following pages. Another beauty with a temperamental growth habit is A. 'Zwartkin', shown on page 77. All of these plants exhibit burgundy red or purple leaf tinting owing to the Zwartkop parentage, and bloom typical of most aeoniums.

Catlin cross (red edges) merging with a green *A. canariense*.

The four plants here are all unidentified, but most likely are either Catlin crosses or similar crosses, whether intentional or via open pollination.

If there are no labels and the owners can't recall where they came from, all bets are off and you get to play 'name that hybrid' and whoever names it with the most authority wins. All are wonderful landscape plants in coastal climates.

The aeoniums seen on this page are plants I spotted and photographed, but were just part of a landscape with no identification. They are almost certainly hybrids, and likely Catlin hybrids due to the influence of *A.* 'Zwartop' for the dark color (the green plant in front of the image at left may be an exception, but might still be a Catlin cross). For example, the group planting below looks like it might be *Aeonium* 'Voodoo', 'Velour', or perhaps 'Garnet'. And even if I show this photo to an expert, they might be a little more sure in their opinion, but they will still leave a little wiggle room in their answer. So as I've said elsewhere, take inspiration from what you see, try to locate and buy a plant that looks like the one you want, or even knock on the owner's door and ask if you can buy or trade for a cutting if you can't find the plant anywhere else. As a nursery owner, I'm advising that as a last resort, but you gotta do what you gotta do.

Above is an old clump growing at the Huntington, called HBG 32644, a Victor Reiter hybrid received in 1974. It frequently forms crests, as seen in the center right of the photo, and in greater detail above right. Below left: a Jack Catlin hybrid of *A.* 'Zwartkop' with *A. tabuliforme*, know as *A.* 'Zwartkin'. More purple that black, it has some of the characteristic flatness of *tabuliforme*, and can grow in a nice, tight clump. It can really change its look and leaf arrangement depending on conditions and time of year, taking almost a brown coloration at times. Another possible name for this plant might be *A.* 'Silk' or 'Silk Pinwheel'. Below right is a drift of *Aeonium* 'Jack Catlin' at the Huntington Gardens, adding a nice color contrast is the *Agave attenuata* 'Boutin's Blue'.

Photos above and below right by John Trager.

Aeoniums at the Huntington Botanical Garden

It can be difficult to distinguish between *A.* 'Zwartkop' and the two darkest, large hybrids. *A.* 'Cyclops' and *A.* 'Voodoo'. All photos on this page are by John Trager of the Huntington, with proper documentation. So I'm taking him at his word, as I doubt I would have got it correct myself. Below and bottom right is *A.* 'Cyclops', which exhibits the largest rosette of the group. Right above and middle are *A.* 'Voodoo', with equally dark foliage in full sun. All of these plants can exhibit the green 'eye' in the center of the rosette depending on amount of sun and time of year. One way to differentiate these hybrids from *A.* 'Zwartop', is that the latter has a shiny, deep, glosy black leaf (some people see red in there, but I'd call it black), and the former cultivars have more of a flat, matte black leaf, sometimes larger and more droopy.

One of my goals with this book was to clear up confusion about similar plants both for you, the reader, and for me, the author and nurseryman that is supposed to be an 'authority' on the subject matter. So I took a February trip to the esteemed Huntington Library and Garden in San Marino, CA, which is, among other things, the foremost public succulent garden in the world. I wanted to see if I could differentiate the various Catlin and similar hybrids. This visit was during a particularly wet winter, and prior to the spring bloom. After a wonderful afternoon of communing with the aeoniums, I can confidently report that I am no more confident than I was before. There are two clumps identified by garden tag as 'Jack Catlin', another as 'Velour', all beautiful, and all look pretty much the same. And later in the year they will all look a little different, perhaps a bit more to the red/black phase, later with more compact rosettes. The staff there can tell the difference between 'Garnet' and 'Velour' and the several 'Jack Catlins', but apart from the very tall 'Cyclops' or the very flat-leaved 'Zwartkin', I'm usually at a loss. So just enjoy them and if you want to figure out what your plant really is, well, good luck.

The tight cluster of *A.* 'Cyclops' (I think) at left grew two years later into the tableau below left, looking like they've stretched their necks, using their cycloptic single eye to look for a way out of their containment and into a new home. I like both versions, but if you prefer the tighter habit, you may need to replace plants every few years.

A cristate flower can sometimes develop out of a non-cristate plant.

An observation that occurred to me after I sent my aloe/agave book off to the printers was that I wished I could be so fortunate as to die like an agave – at the end of my life flowering into a giant 5 times my previous size just in case you didn't know I was here (although leaving my huge dried and mummified corpse on high for all to observe might get a bit morbid after a while). Well, the twin-head *Aeonium* 'Cyclops' lower right are also doing their monocarpic thing with the same type of extraordinary end-of-days celebration. And Thelma and Louise here timed it to go out together.

Aeonium 'Cyclops'

This Catlin cross of *Aeonium* 'Zwartkop' and *A. undulatum* stands apart from the rest of the dark crosses as it reaches a larger size, usually holding a strong green 'eye'. It can reach chest height, and I've seen some then bloom with a several-foot high flower cone, temporarily reaching up over six feet. At a smaller size it can be confused with *A.* 'Voodoo', which is supposedly the exact same cross, but doesn't get quite as tall and can be more of a universal dark coloring. At right is an example of *A.* 'Cyclops' beginning to close itself up in response to summer heat.

Aeonium 'Ballerina'

This small, variegated clustering plant has a nice delicate feel, appearing at a distance to be a garden shrub other than an aeonium or succulent in general. It is thought to be a hybrid of a small species, *Aeonium goochiae*, not often seen in cultivation. The term 'Frosty' sometimes appears with this plant, but may in fact be a different cross.

Aeonium castello-paivae

This small, clustery aeonium is rarely sold as the true species, at least properly identified as such. However, it is likely a parent to several of the named and mostly un-named hybrids in cultivation. The form known as 'Suncup', shown below right, is a variegated form of either the true species, or a cross or cultivar of it.

Aeonium 'Suncup'

This dainty little plant is the variegated form of *Aeonium castello-paivae*, not often seen in cultivation in the regular green form, shown at left. It is a rock/cliff grower in habitat, and would appreciate such a position if planted in-ground, but also makes a nice container plant.

The two plants you see on this page are obviously not the same thing, but what they may share in common is having *Aeonium tabuliforme* as a parent. The larger, thicker-leaved plant below is a long-established garden plant in California, with the other half of its parentage likely being one of the larger aeoniums, such as *A. canariense, urbicum,* or *undulatum*. The smaller plant at left looks even more like a form of tabuliforme, but is obviously crossed with a smaller, clumping aeonium.

Aeonium pseudotabuliforme

Aeonium tabuliforme

This is one of the coolest and most unique of all aeoniums, if not all succulents. As the name suggests, it grows absolutely as flat as a pancake, 'roadkill' style. However, it can be a challenge to grow. In its native Canary Island home, it prefers to grow vertically on rock cliff faces, occupying a niche similar to how many dudleyas grow in California. That can be hard to replicate, so most of us grow them in pots or flat on the ground. When the plant is large enough to reach the edge of the pot, you might need to lift the skirt to get water into the pot. The double head below right is unusual, as it is typically a solitary plant, and will bloom itself into oblivion at maturity, requiring new ones to generally be grown from seed. Below left is an example of one throwing out a crested section.

Aeonium 'Starburst'

This is simply the inverted variegation form of *A.* 'Sunburst', where the yellow is in the middle of the leaf, with the green on the outer edges. Perhaps not quite as bright, but it is an equally stunning plant, with the same basic growth habit.

Occasionally you will find a purely variegated plant, with no green at all, such as the pure yellow-white rosette of *Aeonium* 'Sunburst' seen above. As long as these individuals are still attached to a parent that has other portions with some green to photosynthesize, it will likely survive. But when detached, it may root but becomes much more difficult to grow on its own. This is also the case with other variegated succulents, such as agaves. Right: ten years ago there were relatively few examples of *A.* 'Sunburst' seen in residential or commercial landscapes. The word is out now and it is everywhere.

Inset is the typical rosette elongation/morph of an aeonium into the flower. Since there doesn't appear to be any other rosettes on this plant, it is likely on its last legs. At left is an example of an *Aeonium* 'Sunburst' crest. Typically, as seen here, the crest really compacts the leaves, so the plant is not as colorful, and the dead leaves must be occasionally be pulled out, as they are compressed in so tightly.

Aeonium 'Sunburst'

Its hard not to like this plant. This long-time cultivar is likely a variegated form of *A. davidbramwellii* or a cross with it. It boasts a large, fairly think-leaved rosette, with varying degrees of variegation. Most stems eventually branch with age, and it will reach a height of perhaps 2 feet at most before blooming out. Like most aeoniums, it is fine with full sun in coastal regions, but still benefits from afternoon shade. The cluster above is growing along a short north wall, and gets only early-morning and/or late-afternoon direct sun in winter and seems very happy in this relatively cool and slightly damp location. *A.* 'Sunburst' can be prone to black leaf spotting after extreme heat events. The spots won't heal, but eventually plants will grow out of the ugliness, new leaves slowly replacing the old, damaged ones.

Aeonium simsii

Aeonium simsii is a nice ornamental garden plant, especially when it clusters tightly into mounds as seen here. It is unique among aeoniums in how it flowers laterally from the stem below the rosette, rather than the usual elongation and monocarpic morphing of the rosette itself. The wonderful plants above may in fact be a hybrid of *A. simsii*, as images of the plant in habitat rarely look this nice – although we do tend to baby our plants in cultivation. The rosettes are a bit more round and compact than the true form, which looks more like the mini-hedge at left, photographed at the Ruth Bancroft Garden in Walnut Creek, CA.

Right: a possible *A. simsii cross*, or perhaps just a form of the species with mild tannic striping.

Aeonium 'Cabernet'

An example of some of the wonderful things we humans do when we mess with mother nature – in a good way – is this beautiful cross of *A.* 'Zwartkop' with *A. simsii*. The result is this full, pillowy-growing bush of varying wine-colored and green leaves. Color will vary on time of year and conditions, including an occasional shift from burgundy to a darker purple/black, as seen at left. The only downside to this plant is that it is very sensitive to heat. It can be dicey to grow too far inland without some afternoon shade. Like most aeoniums, it should rebound after winter rains.

Photo: John Trager

Aeonium 'Mardis Gras'

This beautiful plant is a selected cultivar of a variegated hybrid made from other hybrids, identified and isolated by Renee O'Connell of Altman Plants. It has been in the trade for a few years now, but it is rare to see a large specimen, as it seems to be a difficult grower. The image at left was captured by John Trager, and it shows the plant at optimum color and blush. It will go through different phases of coloration depending on conditions and season. The beauty below also exhibits some 'greenhouse happiness'. The example on page 27 shows A. 'Mardis Gras' growing in a more typical semi-neglected state, and how it can change colors due to conditions and time of year.

Aeonuim 'Emerald Ice'

Another engineered beauty by Renee O'Connell, this variegated *A. tabuliforme* cross is a recent introduction but looks to be a winner.

When the single-head, monocarpic form of *Aeonium nobile* reaches maturity and blooms, you can be sad that your plant is slowly going away, but you can also take delight in the wonderful crimson flower explosion you will be treated to for several weeks, typically from spring into early summer.

Aeonium nobile

This is the aeonium that looks least like an aeonium. It has thick, leathery leaves, much more reminiscent of an echeveria, which is what I thought this was when I first encountered it. It is never a common plant, owing to the fact that the true species is a single-head plant, but there is another form now that does multiply, although with somewhat of a less impressive bloom. Younger plants exhibit a tight leaf form, as seen below left. Older plants will sometimes feature long, luxurious older leaves, as seen at left. An individual plant can become surprisingly large. It also has a stunning end-of-days flower, a huge explosion of clustering and tightly packed red/pink little flowers. Unlike many offsetting aeoniums, this is a plant you will have for a number of years, then it will bloom and you won't have it again until you buy a new one, or try to collect the dust-like seeds to start new plants.

If you want to brighten up a darker part of your garden, consider *Aeonium* 'Kiwi'. The form seen at left seems a bit larger than usual, and at the time of this photograph was shifting into a high-yellow phase, yet to exhibit the red edging you can see on the facing page. *Aeonium* 'Kiwi' will color-shift over the seasons, from primarily green with tight yellow 'eyes', to mostly yellow, to yellow with red edging. It can also oscillate from tight to rangy, and sometimes back to tight and full again if you give it time. It can also revert to pure green at times, as seen in the trough planter on the facing page, bottom right.

Above: spring flowers.

Above: This plant has really caught on with the public and the landscaping industry in the past few years, as it makes such a nice complimentary plant in any low-water garden. It maintains a low profile yet will still manage to become a significant drift of color and architecture.

Aeonium 'Kiwi'

This is the most common variegated aeonium, along with A. 'Sunburst'. *A.* 'Kiwi' has a much smaller rosette, but forms dense clusters over time, with a pronounced red leaf blush, usually in the spring. It is thought to be a tricolor variegated version of *A. haworthii*, seen at lower left, which grows larger and is a very low-maintenance 'filler' plant, long-established in many old California gardens and capable of living without outside help. This variegated version apparently was discovered in New Zealand, hence the name 'Kiwi', although the New Zealanders and others call it 'tricolor'. It can offer reversions to green, seen at bottom (which does look a bit different from *A. haworthii* – hence the uncertainty).

This is a fairly large *aeonium*, sometimes called the Giant Velvet Rose, that might be a form of *A. canariense* or *A. palmense*. As the common name implies, it is covered in fine velvety 'hair'. Below is the early stage of bloom, which will eventually elongate into a more conical shape.

Aeonium 'Giant Velvet Rose'

There are a number of bushy non-succulents, annuals or perennials, that can offer spectacular blooming events like this hybrid's yellow winter explosion. But unlike much of that other plant material, an aeonium like the hybrid at left will remain in a tight green ornamental form after the flowers expire, and won't get long and leggy for many years, if at all. The flowers will eventually turn brown and can be clipped back, or the dead sections will eventually be replaced by new growth. Lush beauty and low maintenance – what more can you ask for?

Aeonium 'Alcatraz'

Above: This is supposed to be a cross of *A. nobile* and A. 'Kiwi'. I haven't grown one up enough yet to see it flower, but it looks like it could be a bit of both. I received this cross from John Harvey, so unless somebody has already named it, I'll nominate it as *Aeonium* 'Harv'.

Rudolph Schultz' aeonium book talks about the ancient colonies of aeoniums that have hybridized and gone indigenous on the 'rock' in San Francisco Bay. I visited Alcatraz a while back and saw the plants, and was tempted to slip a piece into my jacket pocket, but I chickened out – I had just taken a jail tour and had a heightened fear of committing a petty crime. Then shortly afterwards, a customer came into my shop and brought me a little start of the aeonium he had lifted from Alcatraz. So now I have a small one, and there is nothing exceptional about it except the story of where it came from.

Aeonium leucoblepharum

This aeonium usually has a dark tannic midstripe, seasonally more visible in the winter and spring. It is endemic to a large swath of eastern Africa, isolated from the majority of aeoniums after the Sahara desert formed, trapping them into cooler, mountainous regions. It does occupy a large range, and is reputed to be variable in form. The primary type seen in cultivation is the attractive striped form seen here. Like most aeoniums, it can really shrink through warm summer months. It has yellow flower clusters in spring, seen inset. The white flowers in the larger image are from a small crassula growing below the aeoniums.

Aeonium smithii

Above: *Aeonium smithii* is very rare in collection, and can be a sensitive grower, almost completely defoliating in the summer heat. It is better treated as a collector plant in a bonsai pot as seen here.

Aeonium 'Lily Pad'

Below is a wonderful and fairly new introduction, *A.* 'Lily Pad'. It is a nice, thick-leaved clustering plant, likely a cross with *A. lindleyi* on the facing page – and it looks like this hybrid is quite an improvement on the species.

Aeonium 'Black Night'

The dark-leaved/green center plant above was one I acquired from a collector some time ago and identified as 'Black Night'. However, most internet searches for that name show images of *A.* 'Zwartkop', which this definitely is not (perhaps a hybrid of?). It has proven to be an excellent garden plant, and hopefully will be more available soon.

Aeonium tortuosum

Left: *Aeonium tortuosum* offers tiny, thick-leaved rosettes that form a dense bush after a time. It is still sometimes known under the genus name '*Aichryson tortuosum*'

Aeonium sedifolium

Above: *Aeonium sedifolium* really doesn't look like an aeonium, with many small, thick heads with a nice olive and red tinge. It is so small it is best as a container plant.

Aeonium lindleyi

All of the small, bushy aeoniums on this page are fairly rare in cultivation, including *A. lindleyi*. Although generally bushy and unremarkable in appearance, it does have the reputation for possessing a juice that is an antidote for the toxic (or at least irritating) sap of euphorbias.

Sempervivum arachnoideum

There are a number of iterations of this 'spider web' sempervivum, above and at left, all sharing the white hairy 'spider web' filaments. They are prolific off-setters, and seem to be among the few that are tolerant of a mediterranean landscape. They are ideally planted among or in the context of rocks, as seen here. Below middle: Sempervivum tectorum has also proved to be an easy grower, at least in dish garden settings. Below right: unidentified hybrid.

Sempervivums

Sempervivums ('live forever') are the classic 'hens and chicks' offsetting rosette plants. Most are from colder climates in eastern Europe, and do better in similar climates. Many are very popular as alpine rockery plants, and very few do well in mediterranean situations. The plants photographed on these pages are all growing in California, and are among the few we can grow. Even these suffer greatly in hot weather. They do tend to grow a little better in the cooler, northern portions of the state.

There also exists a small, 3-member genus of closely related European plants called jovibarba, almost indistinguishable from sempervivums.

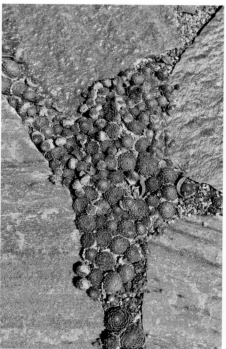

Sempervivums are often hybridized, so with the exception of the few forms I can recognize (*S. tectorum* with burgundy leaf tips, *S. arachnoideum* with its 'spider webbing), I tend not to even attempt to try to identify most that I see. The dainty form of *S. arachnoideum* in the middle image above is growing in a full sun location between pavers, and can handle light foot traffic. I can't think of any other small soft succulent that you can walk on – *Dymondiae margarete* is usually the favored plant for this situation. Congratulations to Mark Reidler for thinking outside the box.

Order: Saxifragales
Family: Crassulaceae
Genus: Echeveria
Species: subsessilis

ECHEVERIAS

Can you find the aeonium hiding in the grower's flat of echeverias and their sub-genera above? I'm pretty sure it is the largest plant on the bottom row – *Aeonium* 'Lily Pad'. Or I could be wrong.

One of the advantages of self-publishing a book is that I don't have an editor telling me not to plug someone else's book. But I'm really hoping that this book is just a jumping-off point for those of you with enough scientific or botanical curiosity to research these plants further. And the best, and really only, books on some of the genera covered here are beautiful labors of love, and I hope you can track these down if you are so inclined. As you might gather from this book, or others I've made, I'm a fan of succulents and nature in general, whether you're learning in book form, or via the internet, or documentaries (Hail David Attenborough!). A few of the books I'm recommending here are sadly out of print, so my hypothetical editor might be okay with this, but I do hope you can find them. It will further your knowledge and improve your bookshelf.

In the Aeonium chapter, I raved about Rudolph Schulz' aeonium book. Perhaps my second favorite succulent book is also by Shulz and Atilla Kapitany, this one about echeveria cultivars (right). It is a noble attempt to catalog the most prominent hybrids and cultivars of this very diverse genus, all gorgeously photographed. But it is over ten years old and there have been a lot of new hybrids introduced since. Cultural tips and grower insights are provided as well. They talk a bit about the true species, but that is really the province of another outstanding book, *The Genus Echeveria* by John Pilbeam (left). It is full of beautiful habitat and cultivation images, with useful information.

Echeveria cante

Echeverias are new world, rosette-forming succulents, primarily from Mexico. You'll hear a few different pronunciations of the genus, which was named in the 1800s after a renowned Mexican botanical illustrator. His name was likely pronounced 'etch-uh-vair- EE-ya', or something close to that, so I don't think the hard 'k' sound, as in 'Ek-uh-VAIR-ee-ya', is correct. But I hear it both ways, so you make the call. Now that that is out of the way . . . these are wonderful, mainly small and compact plants, most better in container culture, but a few of them are strong enough for landscaping in the proper climate. Many are prolific offsetters, often earning the nickname 'hens and chicks', which more appropriately belongs to the sempervivums (that title tends to be given to any plant that multiplies in rosettes). The leaves are thick and fleshy as compared to aeoniums, and echeverias generally don't grow vertically along the central stem the way aeoniums do (there are a few exceptions, particularly the gibbiflora varieties on much thicker stems). As you'll see on the following pages, there are some striking varieties in cultivation with all manner of crinkly and carunculated (there's your new word for the day; see pages 128 - 134 leaves.)

Echeveria colorata in Mexican habitat, looking like an almost too perfectly staged plant

Left:
Echeveria unguicalata

Right:
Echeveria agavoides
'Ebony'

Echeveria lauii

Echeverias in Habitat

Echeverias are primarily native to Mexico, extending into Central and South America. Most are from warmer, summer-wet habitats, but others are from higher elevations and are more cold tolerant. Most occur on vertical topography, often inhabiting crevices in rock faces and outcroppings, similar to dudleyas (and actually quite a few succulents). All habitat photos on this spread by Jeremy Spath.

Echeveria gibbiflora

There are many hybrid cultivars in the genus, accentuating traits that are seen somewhat in nature, but exaggerated in cultivation due to selective breeding. Two of the more striking characteristics that have been developed are the frilly leaved varieties seen at top left, and the bumpy 'carnunculated' leaves exhibited in the plant below it. You'll see more examples on the following pages.

While there are a number of aeonium hybrids that were purposely created, such as the Catlin varieties, aeoniums are notoriously promiscuous and will intermingle and create new garden hybrids on their own. Echeverias aren't quite as loose, and most of the hybrids have been intentional crosses by horticulturists such as Dick Wright, Renee O'Connell, Frank Reinelt, and others. Some of the hybrids date back to European creations from over a hundred years ago. There are by far more echeveria hybrids than true species in cultivation.

Echeverias are related to the genus dudleya, but not quite enough for intergeneric hybridization. However, that doesn't stop some from appearing to be very closely related. Above top are two examples of *Dudleya brittoni*, in front of them is *Echeveria cante*. Both have a white powder on the leaves, with *E. cante* exhibiting a bit more of a purple tint at times, compared to the pure white of the dudleyas. Both are gorgeous plants.

Below is part of a grower's flat of *Echeveria* 'Pearle von Nurnberg'.

Photo by
Michael J. Viray

Above: sometimes you can find botanic beauty in the unexpected details. Here, the stem of a vertical-growing carunculated echeveria shows the pattern formed from where the old leaves were once attached.

Left: an impressive and valuable collection of the superior form of *Echeveria agavoides* 'Ebony'.

Below: an echeveria hybrid, perhaps known as 'Blue Atoll', shows both its propensity to cluster as well as to occasionally form a crest.

Cresting

Cresting (also called 'fasciation') is a growth aberration occasionally seen in succulents, echeverias included. The *E. agavoides* (background) shows an example of stem cresting, where the heart of the growing apex takes on a 'fan' or crested means of growing.

Background: a stem crest of *E. agavoides* 'Beauty'.

Inset above is a crested example of an unidentified echeveria.

Right is a crested show plant specimen of one of the large red echeverias.

Echeveria flowers

The attraction of echeverias is more in their form and leaf color or character, rather than for their flowers. In fact, sometimes the tall flowers are a bit of a liability to the plant, as they can get so tall that they can tilt the plant, and with so much effort going into multiple blooms, (see photo at lower left) the older leaves can fall at an alarming rate, reducing the size of the rosette considerably (it should later grow back to size). And some of the flowers just aren't much to look at. Having said that, quite a few do have nice, colorful flowers, as you can see at right and on the facing page.

Bottom right: *Echeveria peacockii* (or *subsessilis*) in flower. Inset: sometimes even expired flower stalks can look sort of interesting. What were previously orange flowers along the flower stalks have gone black, leaving a cool display. Within a few weeks it will all turn brown and should be removed. Below left is the same variety –– *Echeveria* 'Sahara' in full bloom.

Echeveria agavoides

There are so many iterations of this echeveria – either cultivars, hybrids, perhaps regional forms – that I am no longer sure what the 'type' or original form exactly looks like, but it should be something like the plant above, with thick, light mint-green leaves and often (but not always) some type of red or burgundy leaf edge and tip color. The form above seems to be the species 'type', with a bit less 'lipstick' applied as compared to *E. agavoides* 'Lipstick' as seen on the following pages. All forms will offset at some point, and are fairly hardy plants in cultivation. The variety 'Ebony' seen on the following pages is the most remarkable and desirable among collectors.

On the facing page is just a sampling of some of the *Echeveria agavoides* cultivars and/or hybrids. Top left is the aqua-tinged leaf variety, name unknown. Top middle is 'Romeo'. Top right is the prolific clumping form known as 'Christmas'. Middle left is a red-blushed form. Middle is a giant form. Middle right is un-named with little red tips. Bottom left is possibly 'Maria'. Bottom middle and right are the classic form called 'Beauty'.

Echeveria agavoides 'Lipstick'

Always a favorite is the form of *E. agavoides* with the appropriate name of 'Lipstick'. It is sometimes referred to as 'Corderoy', and is a true species plant from a wild population, selected for its more aggressive red edging. It can make an excellent garden focal point plant, and will provide offsets like most echeverias.

The *E. agavoides* form below is not v. 'Lipstick', but is another pretty blushing charmer, seen here frosted in rain drops. It grows rather large.

Photo credit:
Michael J. Viray.

This beauty is the Cadillac of echeverias, and in fact is one of the most desirable of all succulents. You're a serious succulent collector if you have sought out and procured one of these still fairly rare plants. A six-inch plant still typically will cost over a hundred dollars. It is rare not because of any particular difficulties in growing them, but they are slow to offset, and their owners are reluctant to let their few pups go.

The clone below is the most 'common' form in cultivation, although it is still quite rare. It has a pale green to turquoise skin tone, with deep, dark burgundy leaf tips. Yet I always wondered where the term 'ebony' (black) came from. Then I became aware of the extremely rare clone seen at left, with a lighter green skin but leaf tips that grade from brick red to black (or ebony) leaf tips. This one is so rare it commands a ridiculous price, at least until someone gets it into tissue culture. Something for the wish list.

Echeveria agavoides v. 'Ebony'

According to season and conditions, echeverias – and succulents in general – will change their habit. This particular clump of *E. imbricata* has been very happy in this Cayucos, CA. seaside bowl, to the point of beginning to crowd itself out, and the rosettes are beginning to tighten up in response (water will have a hard time finding its way down into the soil). The rop right rosette has began to shed lower leaves, which is part of a natural progression and not unusual or indicative of a sick plant. You could remove the dead leaves, or better yet, just decapitate that rosette and allow the 'chicks' below to get a little breathing room. And now you have a new 'hen' to grow some more chicks.

Echeveria imbricata

This is a long-established hybrid, dating to late 1800s France. It is a cross of *E. glauca* and *E. gibbiflora* 'Metallica'. The descriptive handle of 'hens and chicks' usually applies to sempervivums, but this clumping echeveria (and some related crosses) also sometimes takes that name, at least in mediterranean climates. It is reputed to be quite cold hardy, and might be one of the most common ornamental succulents in the world. In my experience, you can grow a plant to look full like the one at left, but eventually weather or care conditions will cause heads to at least temporarily shrink, exposing the dead leaves and stems inside. It may grow back into its previous look, or it might not. It might prefer slightly cooler northern California conditions than we have in the south.

Below: I'm sure other echeverias must exhibit this characteristic, but something about *E. imbricata*, perhaps the coating of its skin surface, seems to cause rainwater to collect like mercury in the rosette crown.

There is a beautiful variegated form by the name of 'Compton's Carousel', seen below. However, this is generally a very finicky grower, perhaps preferring life in a greenhouse.

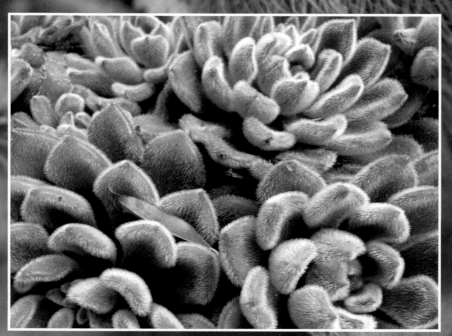

Echeveria 'Doris Taylor'

Perhaps not as striking as the 'Ruby' or other red forms of the fuzzy echeverias, this is nevertheless one of the nicest. It is a very old cross of *E. pulvinata* and *E. setosa*, and has attractive orange flowers in season. It freely offsets, and will at times form a crest, as seen above.

Fuzzy echeverias

There are a handful of true species fuzzy or pubescent echeverias, primarily *E. harmsii* and *E. pulvinata*. There are several other fuzzies (*E. leuchotricha* and *E. coccinea*) that may have some contribution to the hairy hybrids seen in cultivation today. The best and most available forms are probably *E.* 'Doris Taylor' and a few forms of *E. pulvinata* and *E. harmsii* that seasonally exhibit striking ruby red edging, seen at left.

Above: an unidentified plant, possibly an extra fuzzy version of *E.* 'Doris Taylor, or perhaps *E. leucotricha* 'Frosty'.

Left: *E. pulvinata* 'Ruby'.

Right: unidentified plant, perhaps *E. coccinea*, stretching in a low-light situation.

Echeveria pulvinata

There are a few forms of this fuzzy plant, the favorite one being the deep crimson red type seen above – either called 'Ruby', or 'Ruby Slipper', or sometimes 'Red Velvet'. The color will vary on conditions and time of year, generally showing best in the cool winter months. It is a clumper with nice orange flowers, and is sometimes confused with the similar reddish fuzzy *Echeveria harmsii*, which has a similar look but tends to grow more scrappy and floppy over time, or *E. coccinea*, which is variable, sometimes reddish, sometimes not. There is also a silver-white form known as 'Frosty', which may be re-named 'Frigida', in part to avoid confusion with another attractive white fuzzy plant with the same name, *E.* 'Frosty', which is a selected cultivar of *E. leucotricha*. This stuff gets confusing.

An observation that applies to several echeverias, but particularly to this one: you might want to remove the dead flowers on occasion. With a lot of succulents, spent flowers will shrivel and just crumble off if you don't get them first. But I've noticed a large mass planting of one of the red fuzzy *pulvinata* or *harmsii* types in my neighborhood that looks kind of ugly most of the time, and I noticed on further inspection that the plant is fine, it is just semi-covered in dead, crispy brown flower stalks that sort of ruin the look. So as much as we succulent aficionados abhor maintenance, you might want to get on the dead flowers on occasion.

Echeveria setosa

I usually don't use words like 'adorable' for succulents, but if I did, which I'm not, it might apply to *Echeveria setosa*. It has densly packed, tight fuzzy rosettes and nice orange/yellow flowers. Pilbeam's book gives it a good look, showcasing the several varieties, including v. *setosa, v. ciliata, v. deminuta, v. minor,* and *v. oteroi*. And of course there are hybrids too.

Echeveria 'Icycle'

The original hybrid of this plant, intentionally misspelled, is reputed to be a cross of *E. agavoides* and *E. leuchotricha*. Schulz' book says it is mostly solitary, but the form seen now seems to be a vigorous off-setter, so it may be a different hybrid from the one in his book. The form seen here is an excellent garden plant, with silver/mint green leaves and fine hairs that shimmer in the sunlight. Perhaps this variety should be properly spelled 'Icicle' to differentiate if from the first hybrid.

Echeveria shaviana

The forms of this echeveria in cultivation are usually either cultivars or hybrids of the species plant. One is called 'Pink Frills', which looks like the plant at left and is a naturally occurring sport in the wild. Altman Plants has introduced a new version called 'Neon Breakers' (at right)which is supposed to be more durable and disease resistant than the others. The true species form looks more like the plant at left, with varying degrees of leaf frilliness. It is a frequent contributor to new hybrids.

Echeveria 'Perle von Nurnberg'

You will see this plant spelled a few different ways, but I'm defaulting to Rudolph Schulz' version here. It is an old German hybrid of *E. gibbiflora* and *E. elegans*. It is slow to offset, but if it finds a happy place, it offers a splash of almost incandescent lavender-purple to your garden or arrangement. It shares a leaf coloration with E. 'Afterglow' on the facing page, but is smaller with thicker leaves.

Echeveria 'Afterglow'

This stunner is a large growing and enduring cross of *E. cante* and *E. shaviana*, originally done by Bay Area grower Don Worth. It has a slightly different sister seedling of the same cross named *E.* 'Morning Light'. The lavender pink leaves can vary in hue depending on time of year. It can offset with age, and is one of the echeverias that might benefit by cutting off excessive flowers, which can tax the plant somewhat and cause leaf shedding. This looks like a dainty grower, but is actually quite hardy and cold tolerant.

This beauty may be a cross of or cultivar of *E. gigantea*. As the name suggests, it is a big one, sometimes characterized by the frilly leaves of the closely related *E. gibbiflora*. This particular plant has been isolated by a collector for future propagation. I put my name on the list, as I find it sort of mesmerizing. I actually find quite a few succulents mesmerizing. Maybe I should have that checked out.

Echeveria gibbiflora

This is a variable species in habitat, with many derivatives and hybrids in cultivation. Most of the large carunculated plants on the following pages were created from some form of this plant. The large plants above appear to be close to the species type called 'Violescens' or 'Metallica'. The cluster growing at right in a commercial property in Santa Cruz, CA, appears to be be a gibbiflora cross as well.

The Crinkly & Carunculated

These two wonderful aberrations create stunning plants. Original species *E. gibbiflora* that naturally display just a hint of a trait have been crossed and back-crossed over the years to form many wonderful 'crinkly' or 'cabbage-like' leaf edges. California grower Dick Wright was one of the earliest to experiment with these plants, and is still creating new plants today, over fifty years after his first crosses. Carunculations are the leprosy-like 'growths' on the leaves of many of these plants, beautiful to most of us, hideous to the unenlightened. One of the original carunculated hybrids was called 'Paul Bunyan', but there have been many derivations and permutations created since. Check out Dick and Craig Wright's 'Bubble Machine' on page 133. Most of these are large-growing plants, some growing upright on stems over time.

Growing equally large and almost as bizarre are some of the 'cabbage-leaved' or 'crinkly' echeverias, such as the specimen at right. There are many named varieties, such as 'Pink Frills', but identification can be difficult, so in this book I'm mostly not even going to try to identify them individually. These are just carunculated or crinkly hybrids.

Top left is the Dick Wright hybrid known as 'Culibra', a highly carunculated plant, characterized by its rolled, tube-like leaf openings. Above right and below left are two heavily carnculated crosses, both somewhat resembling the hybrid 'Etna'. Below middle is unidentified, perhaps *E*. 'Crinkles' or *E*. 'Aquarius'. Bottom right: unidentified, possibly *E*. 'Alma Wilson'.

Echeveria leaves can have a quality almost reminiscent of rubber or latex. In this example, an older leave begins to take on an eerie translucence as it begins to die off.

Most of the beauties and beasties on this page were hybridized by Dick Wright, seen here with his son and co-propagator Craig. Dick began experimenting with echeveria hybrids when he lived in Los Angeles in the sixties, and continued upon his move to rural Fallbrook near San Diego in the seventies. He barely survived a wildfire in 1996, but lost almost all of his collection. Undaunted, he started again and now has a whole host of new plants to his credit, and an international waiting list to get them. One of the more striking introductions is called "Bubble Machine', seen on the facing page.

A Frankenstein's monster of a plant, *Echeveria* 'Bubble Machine' is either a true beauty of genetic manipulation, or an example of man's inhumanity to plant.

Echeveria 'Sahara'

This is a particularly robust cross. It has a blue to neon pink cast, with leaves that are crinkly, but not as extreme as some of the other crosses. However, it tends to stay more compact and doesn't elongate as much along the central stem, offsetting tightly with age. It is also more tolerant of hot and cold conditions, making it one of the best echeverias for the landscape. It is also a showy bloomer. It was formerly called *E.* 'Lotus'.

Echeveria 'Big Red'

This long-stemmed, copper-red plant may in fact be one of several hybrids. 'Big Red' seems like a fitting name, but this might also be *E. fimbriata v. fasciculata*, or E. 'Clarence Wright', or even a cultivar of the species plant *E. fimbriata* called 'Mahogany Rose', which has more rounded, spade-shaped leaves. The plant identified as 'Big Red' in Schulz' book looks a little different.

Whatever it is, this form commonly seen in cultivation is a large-growing, rambling plant that may need to be cut back on occasion, as it can grow itself into an awkward form, as seen in above inset (which is also forming a crest). Most of the large carunculated and frilly plants seen on the previous pages can also end up this way over time. As you can also see at right and on page 111, it is prone to forming a crest, which is the most interesting and desirable form. Like most red plants, it needs some sun to keep the color.

Renee O'Connell is a renowned hybridizer on the staff of Altman Plants, and she has contributed a number of established hybrids, echeverias and otherwise, including most if not all of the plants on this page. Sometimes a crowded grower's flat, while obviously planted more densely than you would ordinarily space them, has a nice

compressed feel.

Above left: a nicely formed and staged crested example of *Echeveria pulidonis*. Courtesy of Tina Zucker.

Above right: *Echeveria* 'Andromeda' is another new *E. shaviana* cross that appears to be an excellent landscape plant.

Below left: *Echeveria* 'Blue'Sky' is a durable, landscape-friendly plant. As the name applies, it has a nice blue tint, and looks somewhat like a wide-leaved cross of *E. imbricata*.

Below right: *Echeveria* 'Encantada' is a large, robust hybrid.

Echeveria subrigida

Not an easy plant to find, this stunner features white leaves with red edging, and has been used to create some of the more attractive echeveria hybrids. A true species plant, it rarely offsets and must be grown from seed, which always means such a plant will not be as available as some of the more cooperative multipliers. Like *E. cante*, it seems to be a touchy plant in cultivation, at least in most parts of California. The main difficulty with both plants seems to be flower-related. Like all echeverias, a lot of effort goes into flower production, sometimes at the expense of the plant. These plants really seem to sacrifice themselves at blooming time (see facing page), so despite the nice inflorescence, you might want to try cutting the blossoms early to keep the plant happy. Also known by an occasional grower's name of 'Fire and Ice', it is one of the finest in the genus, and worth a try if you can find one.

Below is a rare example of a crested specimen of *E. subrigida*.

Echeveria cante

Echeveria cante is one of the most beautiful, yet difficult to grow plants in the genus. It features smooth, powdery, white/purple leaves, a bit like some of the nicer dudleyas. Only rarely available as it is a non off-setter, seed raised greenhouse specimens can look like the plant above for a year or two, but often end up looking more like the plant near left. It may well come back, but it will take a while. Sometimes that may be the result of post-bloom fatigue – the same plant is shown at far left six months prior in bloom – but regardless of conditions, most *E. cante* I'm aware of go through progressive periods of renewal and degradation. I wouldn't recommend this plant for in-ground planting, but perhaps in a pot you can find a happy place for it.

Echeveria elegans

There are several forms of *Echeveria elegans*, with the prolific, small-rosette form seen above being one of the most common. There is a larger form as well, also an enthusiastic clumper.

Echeveria runyonii 'Topsy Turvy'

The true type of *Echeveria runyonii* with more typical leaves is rarely seen, or at least properly identified, in cultivation (The plant on page 153 may be a *runyonii* cross). Rather, the unusual-leaved form christened 'Topsy Turvy', seen above, is the most encountered form. Below left is an unusual cultivar or hybrid, perhaps called 'Longfingers'. Below right is a fantastic cultivar called 'Cubic Frost', or sometimes just 'Cubic', with more compact and geometrically arranged leaves. Below middle is a nice overgrown grower's flat of the plant that needs thinning out.

Echeveria 'Cubic Frost'

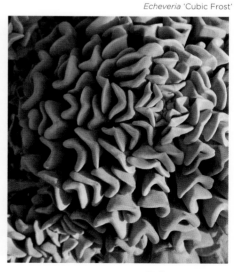

Echeveria 'Monet'

Echeveria 'Monet' is a large, robust hybrid of E. colorata (facing page). Fairly new to the trade, it appears to be an excellent landscape plant with a beautiful blue-purple cast.

Echeveria chihuahuaensis

E. chihuahuaensis is another variable and sometimes hybridized plant, similar to E. colorata but smaller and sometimes a more aggressive offsetter. It is usually characterized by red-dipped leaf tips.

Echeveria colorata 'Mexican Giant'

There are a number of forms of *Echeveria colorata*, but one of the best is known as the 'Mexican Giant' (although almost all echeverias are from Mexico). The 'giant' label is appropriate, as this clone can grow to over a foot and a half in diameter. Its' ghostly pale purple-blue coloring is appealing. My friend Joe commented that on a full moon night, this was the one plant in his dark backyard full of succulents that just seemed to illuminate itself in the moonlight. It has very thick leaves, similar to a graptopetalum or pachyphytum.

Echeveria peacockii / subsessilis

The true species form of *E. peacockii* looks a bit different from the plants seen here, with less truncated leaves and more of a solitary growth habit. Seen here may in fact be forms of *E. subsessilis*, which has since been subsumed into *E. peacockii*. Not always properly identified, or even identified at all by growers, this plant, whatever it is, has pointed tips to its blue leaves, and often has a geometric form as seen at left.

This is likely an *Echeveria runyonii* hybrid, growing in-ground in a south-facing decomposed granite wall. Subdued color, but wonderful design.

Echeveria 'Moondust', a cross of the finicky grower *E. laui* with the more durable *E. lilacina*.

Echeveria nodulosa 'Painted Beauty'

Echeveria nodulosa 'Banitsukasa'

I wish I could tell you that the glorious painted plant above left was an easy grower, but since this species' introduction, I've found that once out of the greenhouse, it begins to go south and seldom approaches the original outrageous look. The form 'Banitsukasa' above right was a surprise to me, obviously a new cultivar or perhaps hybrid of what appears to be Asian origin, but at press time I have little information on this plant, other than that I hope it is a better grower than the true form.

Echeveria 'Lola'

Above: *Echeveria* 'Lola' is a gorgeous Dick Wright hybrid, a cross of *E. lilacina* and *E. derenbergii*. It is usually solitarty, but can offset with age. It can be a temperamental grower, but worth the effort.

Below center: *Echeveria lilacina*
Below left and right: unidentified beauties.

Echeveria lauii (x?)

Echeveria Cuspidata v. gemmula or 'zaragosa'?

The little beauties on this page are various collector echeverias, photographed on a trip to a private collector's yard. Many are crosses of or superior forms of *E. colorata*, *E. agavoides*, *E. cuspidata* and *E. chihuahuaensis*. All are fairly rare clones and at present demand a pretty good price via ebay. Most of these rarities find their way into broader availability at lower prices over a period of time, especially if a grower puts it into tissue culture.

Echeveria 'Romeo' (x?)

Echeveria 'Sirius'?

The subtle beauty above is probably a hybrid by Frank Reinelt of Capitola, CA. He made quite a few winners, and the plant above is likely a cross of *E. agavoides* and *E. colorata*.

Above left is *Echeveria* 'Blue Bird' by Frank Reinelt. It has nice, fat, glaucous leaves that form red tips and edges in fall and winter. Above right is a variegated example of *Echeveria* 'Black Prince'. Below left is an unidentified Dick Wright hybrid, and below right is a Frant Reinelt cross, likely involving *E. agavoides* and *E. colorata*.

There are some rare and expensive collector echeverias in the flat above. This image and some of the plants on the preceding few pages were taken at a collector/propagator's house. Collectors have a discriminating eye for beauty and nuance in the plant world, and are at the forefront of creating new gems that will eventually make their way into our hands. Some start out expensive and the price eventually comes down. Sometimes not.

Above and top right: permutations of *E.* 'Raindrop', a very popular plant with collectors.

Below right: A clumping green cultivar, possible named *E.* 'Sinjen', after a long-time San Diego area horticulturist.

Below: *Echeveria pallida* is one of the few green echeverias in cultivation.

At left is the clustering, small-rosette species *Echeveria* 'Set-Oliver'. It can be a vigorous clumper and is a nice landscape accent plant. The hybrids above and below are unidentified, but a guess on the plant above might be 'Violet Queen', and the plant below might be a cross or form of *E. peacockii*.

Echeveria 'Set – Oliver'

Above is *Echeveria lutea*, still rare in captivity as it rarely if ever offsets, boasting some of the most stunning and uniquely yellow flowers of the genus. It also has a very distinct thin and channeled leaf. Below left is the tiny *Echeveria purpusorum*, a unique plant sometimes mistakenly categorized as a graptopetalum or pachyphytum. It is a parent to some nice hybrids. Below right is *Echeveria* 'Black Knight', an *E. affinis* sport with dark coloration, slightly longer of leaf than E. 'Black Prince', a hybrid by Frank Reinelt.

Above left is a highly prized variegated form of *Echeveria subsessilis*. Above right is unidentifed, perhaps *E. pulidonis*. Below left is *E.* 'Bluebird, and below right is unidentified but looks like the species form of *E. runyonii*.

Order: Saxifrageles
Family: Crassulaceae
Genus: Pachyphytum
Speices: oviferum

GRAPTOPETALUMS and PACHYPHYTUMS

and graptosedums and pachyverias and sedeverias and graptoverias . . .

Graptopetalum hybrid

Pachyphytum compactum

Pachyphytum oviferum
Photo: Jeremy Spath

D
on't feel bad if you're having trouble identifying or even differentiating between these plants. I'm in the business and I get confused all the time. They all have fat, inflated and fleshy leaves, usually clustering rosettes. Some of the more popular forms I can tell on sight, but quite a few I'll look at and think 'Yeah, that's a pachy-grapto, grapto-pachy thingy, maybe a cross with a sedum or echeveria . . .'. They can look alike.

Both of these genera are primarily Mexican natives, related closely enough to echeverias that there are quite a few intergeneric crosses of both with echeverias. These are called graptoverias and pachyverias, and there are also some sedum/echeveria crosses called, you guessed it, sedeverias and graptosedums. The result is that there are a whole bunch of wonderful fat-leaved, clustering rosette succulents that can be very difficult to identify. At the time of this writing, I have owned a succulent nursery for 25 years and I had to really do my homework to identify many of the plants here, and I apologize if I still might have a few wrong in this brief sample I'm showing you.

Pachyphytums ('fat-leaved') have universally fat, inflated-looking leaves. Graptopetalums do as well, although in general their leaves exhibit more of a pointed tip. All are easily propagated by separating a rosette with a bit of stem. Even without planting in soil, roots should form within a week or two. Many will sport new growth from the base of a separated leaf. Once you have one, you really don't need to buy any more if you make just a token effort at propagation. But please support your local nursery – there will always be a new type to try.

Pachyphytum compactum

Pachyphytum compactum is one of several plants sometimes referred to as 'little jewel' or 'little gem'. In this case, that is an apt moniker. It has a remarkable 'carved' leaf pattern. Still rare in cultivation, some have a red-pink blush as well. The form at left really does look like it came out of a jewel box.

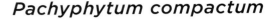

Pachyphytum viride

There is not a lot of information out there on this fairly obscure pachyphytum. It is a true species with yellow-green leaves, that can blush to pinkish red under certain conditions. It does have a showy white flower.

Pachyphytum oviferum

Graptopetalum amethystenum

Pachyphytum oviferum vs. Graptopetalum amethystenum

Pachyphytum oviferum looks so much like *Graptopetalum amethystenum* (formerly identified by most as *Pachyphytum amethystenum*) that it really seems wrong that they are in different genera. But they do indeed have completely different flower structures – *G. amythystenum* with the 5-point star flower vs. the scorpioid (shaped like a scorpion's arching tail – I love that word) flower with closed, bell-shaped pachyphytum blooms as seen above right. *Grapatopetalum amethystenum* has a pink/amethyst color as the name implies, but *P. oviferum* can range from blue to light pink/purple to almost a ghostly white. From my observation, *P. oviferum* is the better and more vigorous grower, better suited for landscape applications if that is your intent. These softies have to be among the absolutely softest and least threatening of all the plants in this book.

Pachyphytum oviferum

Graptoveria 'Fred Ives'

This is one of the most vigorous succulents in cultivation. It is an old cross of *Graptopetalum paraguayensis* (facing page), with an echeveria, done in England over 80 years ago and named after a prominent horticulturist of the day. It has a large rosette and freely clusters, and frequently will form crests. The color can range from a vibrant pink/purple as seen here, with older leaves fading to a brownish-suede, as seen below left, giving it a two-tone color scheme. It is among the easiest growers in this group, fantastic as a landscape repetition plant.

Graptopetalum paraguayensis

This wonderful and ubiquitous – and somewhat variable – clumper isn't really from Paraguay – it is from Mexico. Apparently there was a mislabeled crate on a delivery a hundred years ago and the wrong name stuck. It is generally a bluish to ghostly pink plant, although old leaves can rust into a brownish orange as seen at right. It will grow thick and full, or cascade out of a pot and get leggy, in a good way, as above. It is probably the easiest succulent to propagate. Break off a rosette and if it doesn't already have little hairy roots, they will develop quickly. The inset image shows the variability in coloration.

Graptopetalum pachyphyllum

This is an excellent, tightly clumping plant that can vary from green, above right, to bluish with pink blushing, seen above left. It is great in-ground or in containers. It is also identified at times as belonging to the entirely different sedum genus.

Graptopetalum filiferum

This perfect looking little creature is undoubtedly the model for a number of the fake realistic-looking plastic or silk succulents. Rosettes are generally small, up to 5 inches across. It may have gone through a few reclassifications, as it is sometimes identified as *Echeveria filiferum*. There is an excellent intergeneric hybrid between *G. filiferum* and *Echeveria agavoides* called *Graptoveria* 'Silver Star'.

Graptoveria 'Opalina'

One of the more beautiful and enduring hybrids is *Graptoveria* 'Opalina', a Robert Grimm cross of *Echeveria colorata* and *Graptopetalum amethystinum*. Its' opalescent shifting hues are reminiscent of the latter, but its rosette size comes from the echeveria side of the family. It will cluster in a clump on the ground, or if it can make it over the side of a pot as seet at left, it will begin to cluster along a cascading stem. As with most plants of color, the sun will bring out the pink hues, and it will fade to more of a blue or greenish tint in the shade. Below is an extra plump cultivar that will hopefully soon become available.

Graptosedum 'Vera Higgins'

This little red-bronze clumper is one of the better intergeneric crosses, in this case between *G. paraguayensis* and *Sedum stahlii*. Older leaves tend to persist along the stem, giving it a two-tone appearance. It is named after renowned British horticultural artist Vera Higgnis.

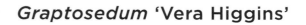

Graptoveria 'Debbie'

This is a lovely plant with a nice, frosty pink-purple leaf color. It looks a bit like *Echeveria* 'Pearle von Nurnberg' but with much more inflated leaves, and more of a clustering habit. The small blue-green plant in front is *Sedum clavatum*.

Graptosedum 'California Sunset'

Top: Graptosedum 'California Sunset' looks qute a bit like a combination of its two parents – *Graptopetalum paraguayensis* and *Sedum adolphii*.

I have no idea what the grapto-pachy thingy is above, but it is' variegated and thus rare and probably commands a high price.

Sedeveria letizia

You can't get a much brighter red in a succulent than the outer leaf edges of this plant if grown in sun and especially during cool winter conditions, as at right. It will not occupy a large space, but is excellent in pockets of a rock garden or sharing space in a combined succulent bowl. The image above shows the plants greening up and beginning to flower in early spring.

Order: Saxifragales
Family: Crassulaceae
Genus: Dudleya
Species: pulverulenta x brittonii

Photo by Jeremy Spath

DUDLEYAS

Dudleyas are some of the most beautiful of the soft succulents, but only a handful are often propagated. Being California and northern Baja natives, they are near and dear to many of us succulent aficionados. Most of the great ornamental succulents in cultivation are from Africa and Mexico, so we are proud of one of our few native ornamental succulent genera. Due to their scarcity and the fact that they are not yet major players in the trade, I'm probably devoting a few too many pages here to the genus, but they are soft succulents, and are some of my absolute favorite plants. Plus, we are able to venture not too far from home and see them in their native habitat. If you live in California, get out there and go dudleya hunting. It's a great excuse to get outside and into nature. But please just take photos or seed, not plants.

Dudleya pachyphtum inhabits a very limited slice of island habitat in Baja. Photo by Jeremy Spath.

Above: dudleyas are generally best as landscape plants in California, but many can be happily kept in containers as well.

Until the rumored new dudleya book arrives, the only book on the genus to my knowledge is a self-published effort by the late Paul Thomson from the early 80s. It is a labor of love, text typed on what looked like an antique typewriter, with color plates in the middle. The information is the best available at the time, but much has changed over the years, and there were a number of inaccuracies. Nevertheless, it is a collector's item for plant geeks, and there are some nice images.

The best and most authoritative treatment to date is the Volume 76, November 2004 issue of the Cactus and Succulent Journal, wherein they broke with the usual format and dedicated an entire issue to one genus. It has great images, thorough and accurate information, with articles by Kelly Griffin, Steve McCabe, Julia Etter and several others intimate with the group. Let's hope Mssrs. Griffin, McCabe and Jeremy Spath get off the schnide and get their new dudleya book done. I know they're holding wonderful images, and I've been on a dudleya field expedition with these guys. They climb mountains for their little babies.

At my succulent nursery in southern California, I will occasionally encounter folks that are new to succulents and assume I 'go out to the desert' to get all my succulents. The truth is that is illegal and unethical, and most of the plants at my nursery are indigenous to Africa and Mexico and other more mediterranean areas of the world. We sadly have very few native succulents from southern California that have much ornamental value. Other than a few agaves and cacti that are mostly found in the desert areas of the state, just about the only native succulent group we have of any renown are the dudleyas. And many of those don't have much of a visual attraction either, but there are a few. Dudleyas range from northern California into Baja, and the most prized are some of the powder-white varieties, such as *D. brittonii* (above). Dudleyas are one of several plant groups known as 'live forevers'. Most pronounce it 'DUD-lee-ya', sometimes 'dud-LAY-uh'.

Dudleyas are generally easy to grow (they are our natives after all), requiring virtually no water out of our rainy season (although many will accept some summer irrigation). However, some of the most prized dudleyas are difficult to obtain, not due to being poor growers, but because they are non off-setters and seed collection and germination is a laborious process that most commercial growers don't want to hassle with. The seed is as small and fine as dust. It can take a year or two to get them up to a salable size. So we often rely on the inveterate backyard grower/enthusiast to bring some of these plants to market. If you find a *Dudleya pachyphytum* for sale, be sure it was a seed-started plant, and if so, buy it and try to propagate it.

Dudleyas 169

Dudleyas 171

Photos: Jeremy Spath

Above: *Dudleya brittonii* in habitat, Baja, CA.

Left: *D. brittonii* in bloom.

Right: *D. brittonii* cross with *D. pulverulenta*.

Dudleya brittonii

This is arguably the most desirable of the available dudleyas. Native to the northern Baja coast right up to the California border, the most popular form is a bright white, large rosette, with large pink flower stems in the spring. It is similar to its southern California cousin *Dudleya pulverulenta*, but is thicker and a bit more of a statement plant.

This plant rarely bifurcates into more than one head (although there are hybrids that look much like it that will clump). In habitat it mostly grows vertically on cliffs, but it will also grow on flat ground. Being coastal, it is more tolerant of summer water or moisture than *D. pulverulenta*, and is a better candidate for cultivation. When you see it as a cluster, most likely these were seedlings growing around the mother plant. Although there are two 'i's at the end of the species name, it is generally pronounced 'britton-eye', rather than 'brittone-ee-eye', which is what we often do with Latin names with the double 'i'. But either works.

The plant in front/lower position in the image at left exhibits a truncated, folded-over leaf habit. I'm not sure if this is a regional variety, a genetic aberration, a hybrid or what – but I like it. The more common form is seen in the image above or on the opposite page.

The green form of *Dudleya brittonii* (right) like the white form, does well on vertical rock surfaces. One advantage of this predilection is that it will help keep small and isolated populations from excessive predation.

Photo: Viggo Gram

Left: a cliffside cluster of *D. brittonii* with an ocean view in northern Baja. It has a narrow native range, but is very abundant where it does exist. Much of the reason for this is that the remaining populations are mostly growing high on inaccessible cliffs, and are additionally protected by agaves and cacti.

Dudleya pulverulenta

One of the few striking ornamental succulents from California, *Dudleya pulverulenta* ranges from Northern Baja to Central California. Sometimes called the 'chalk rose', this powder-white rosette is similar to *D. brittonii*, the main difference being that this plant has thinner leaves. Like most dudleyas, it will shrink and contract through the dry summer and fall seasons, and looks best after winter rains. It likes to grow in vertical, rocky situations, often on north-facing slopes. Some of the best populations of *Dudleya pulverulenta* are colonies that have inhabited road cuts in rocky, decomposed granite soil.

Left inset: the temporary circular banding effect is from water pooling in the rosette.

Despite being a native, this is a more difficult plant to keep in cultivation that *D. brittonii*. The latter is more of a coastal plant, used to more moisture, and will accept summer watering. *D. pulverulenta* really wants to be left alone in the dry season, and will naturally shrink back dramatically over the late summer and into fall. Leaves will shrink and become paper thin, but you need to leave it alone. If you have a more vertical in-ground planting situation, this is your plant.

Although not yet exactly rare or endangered in California, let's please keep it that way – don't field collect. Just take photos like I did here. Sadly, most dudleyas, including this one, are rarely propagated for sale. If you do find one, or several, plant them in proximity with each other, as I have found they will germinate without our assistance, and you might find baby plants below the parent after a period of time (see image on page 44). We need to propagate more dudleyas!

Dudleya
pulverulenta x
D. brittonii

This spectacular plant is a hybrid of *D. pulverulenta* and *D. brittonii*, and grows huge. This dudleya is over 20 inches across, and will appear even larger after all the new flowers reach several feet in height. The leaf patterning is a natural result of rainwater collecting on the leaves and diluting the 'chalk' leaf covering. At other times it is more of a pure white. This cross is not yet common in cultivation, but hopefully will be someday, as it is a more vigorous grower than *D. pulverulenta*, which despite being a southern Calfornia native, will really suffer from any incidental off-season watering. As much as it looks like there is a ring of off-setting new plants emerging around the rosette at right, these are actually the early stages of what will be 3-foot high flower stalks.

Dudleya candida might be one of the finest ornamental plants in the genus, but is still rare in collections. It may be a close cousin to *D. brittonii*, and looks a bit like *D. greenii*. Endemic to a few restricted and small islands off the coast of northern Baja, it needs to be propagated more. I'm working on it.

Dudleya candida

Bottom Photos: Viggo Gram

Dudleya anthonyi

The plant above is *Dudleya anthonyi*, almost indistinguishable from *D. brittonii*, differing primarily in flower and usually more thin-leaved, and much more rare. It is highly valued by collectors. The habitat plant above, photographed by Jeremy Spath, is a thicker-leaved iteration. It is endemic to an island off of northern Baja, with a small mainland population.

Dudleya greenei

This Channel Islands native is a variable white, clustering plant. There is a dwarf form, also known as *Dudleya gnoma* or 'White Sprite', seen at bottom left. There are some hybrids of this plant out there, likely crossed with *D. attenuata*, which produces a white clumper that looks more like the latter.

Dudleya brittonii flower
Photo by Viggo Gram

This powder-white beauty is likely a cross of *Dudleya pachyphytum* and *Dudleya anthonyi*, both rare in cultivation. Each plant is endemic to its own island off of the Pacific coast of Baja, too far apart to come into contact and hybridize naturally. But of course we botanically curious humans like to have fun with plants, leading to new creatures such as this, created at UC Santa Cruz by top dudleya guy Steve McCabe.

While most of the colorful succulents in this book are from faraway lands, we still do have some less-loved succulents from California, such as *Dudleya edulis*, shown growing in habitat at left. This particular habitat is a short walk from my house, on a steep sandstone bluff between two streets and close to a gas station and a freeway offramp. This little compromised and hopelessly fragmented and isolated – but fortunately mostly inaccessible – slice of nature has both *D. edulis* and *D. pulverulenta* coexisting with our small native mammilaria and a nasty form of native opuntia, along with an abundance of African 'ice plants' and weeds, and some native bushes. Like racoons and opossums, our native succulents have dug their heels in and have learned to live alongside the newcomers in such small slices of undisturbed but compromised original habitat. Maybe this isn't growing the way nature intended, but nature still finds a way.

Dudleya edulis and most of the other Southern California dudlyas, lacking much ornamental 'zing', are seldom propagated or available for sale. Their more dull-green color and sometimes sloppy or weedy-looking growth habit works in their favor. Please leave them in habitat, or try to collect seed and grow your own. As the name implies, it is edible and was part of the diet of the indigenous people of the area. Most dudleyas love growing on steep rocky slopes and ledges such as this, and this might be their saving grace to avoid predation or death by development. Hang in there babies.

The cute little trio at left is probably a group of *Dudleya farinosa*, a central California native, seen here staged in a planter bed at Succulent Gardens Nursery in Watsonville, CA.

Dudleya pachyphytum

Endemic to one island off of the Pacific coast of Baja, this dudleya is unique in appearance due its fat leaves. The literal translation from Latin for pachyphytum is 'fat leaves', which is also the genus name for the distantly related plants from mainland Mexico covered earlier in this book. It is exceedingly rare in collection, and also in its very limited native habitat. All plants in cultivation are hopefully seed-started. Care is similar to most other dudleyas, and seems to be shy about too much summer water. I lost the one specimen I had years ago, probably due to overwatering in the dry season. You think you're doing them a favor . . .

Photo: Jeremy Spath

'Finger- leaved' Dudleyas

'Finger-leaved' is only a visual category, but there a number of dudleyas that would match that description. I have a feeling that most of the unidentified plants seen here, which are the most likely (and nicest) forms seen available for sale, are hybrids that might be any combination of *D. caespitosa*, *D. hassei, D. greenei,* or *D. attenuata*. Flower time is usually spring, with nice clusters of white to yellow-gold small flowers on equally interesting red/ pink racemes.

Dudleya caespitosa

Known appropriately as the Coast Dudleya or more confusingly as 'Sea Lettuce', *D. caespitosa*'s native range hugs the coast primarily from Los Angeles to Monterey counties. It prefers to grow vertically in rocky or sandy situations, but is fine in a pot with minimal outside help. The habitat images here are the real deal, photographed by Jeremy Spath, but you can tell that the hybrids on the previous pages probably have some of this plant in them.

Dudleya virens
ssp. *hassei*

Catalina Island dudleya

Crassulaceae

www.learningpinearboretum.calpoly.edu

Dudleya virens ssp. hassei

From what I've gathered, there are several forms of *D. virens*, but subspecies *hassei* seems to be the favored ornamental form. The identified clump at left is growing at the botanic garden at Cal Poly San Luis Obispo, the specimen above at the San Diego C&S Show.

Photo by
Ruud de Block, Hortus Botanicus,
Amsterdam, Holland

Duleya farinosa

There is tremendous variability among dudleyas even within the same species, and *D. farinosa* is a case in point. It can be thin-leaved, fat-leaved, white or green, prone to clump or maybe not. I'm sure there have been some battles between lumpers and splitters with this plant and probably the whole genus. *D. farinosa* shares habitat with *D. caespitosa,* also clinging to the central California coast, with this one having a common name of 'bluff lettuce'. I don't get the 'lettuce' moniker for dudleyas.

The plants at left are growing on an adobe hillside at a wholesale nursery. I was convinced that they were a type of dudleya, but in fact are *Echeveria lutea*, an example of convergent evolution.

Order: Saxifragales
Family: Crassulaceae
Genus: Crassula
Species: falcata
'Morgan's Beauty'.

CRASSULAS

Crassula capitella ssp. thyrsiflora 'Red Pagoda' at left; *Crassula* 'Campfire' right.

Crassulas in Habitat

Most members of the crassula group in cultivation are of African origin, and are happy in most mediterranean climates. The habitat images on this page were taken in situ by Jeremy Spath. This image is a nicely spiraling form of *Crassula rupestris*. Bottom left is a favorite, *Crassula arborescens*, also known as 'Silver Dollar Jade'. Below right is likely *Crassula hemisphaerica*.

We need to be a little specific with the botany here. This section is about the genus crassula, within the family crassulaceae (sometimes referred to as 'stonecrop'), of which most of the plants in this book belong to. Aeoniums, sempervivums, echeverias, dudleyas, pachyphytums, senecios, kalanchoes, sedums, cotyledons – a huge number of the cultivated soft succulents, reside within the broader family of crassulaceae. But the eponymous and representative group for our purposes in this section is the genus crassula, including the 'jades' and a series of 'stacked' or bushy varieties.

Many crassulas, particularly the 'stacked' varieties, have a somewhat monocarpic bloom. Much like aeoniums, individual rosettes or heads will in season (usually spring but not exclusively) elongate into tall flower spires, as seen with the *Crassula capitella* 'Campfire' below or the *Crassula perforata* at left. At the end of the bloom, you will have a lot of brown, dead material to cut off, or you can do nothing and it will eventually blow away, with new plant material now growing compactly beneath it.

This phenomenon is really pronounced with the amazing red *Crassula capitella* 'Red Pagoda' on the previous introduction page, so much so that I hesitate to recommend the plant. The photo is a bit of a tease, as the compact stage seen there is fleeting. Both of those hot-colored crassulas will soon begin to elongate, and after blooming out can look pathetic. The color of the Pagoda usually reverts to green for quite a period of time as well, but eventually new, compact growth will emerge from beneath the chaos and you can hope for a return to glory for a brief time the following spring.

Left: *Crassula capitella* 'Campfire' in elongated winter bloom and full blazing orange coloration.

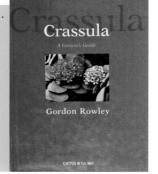

Sorry to tease you with another out-of-print treasure, but this book by Gordon Rowley is the definitive tome on the genus. Thoroughly researched and written by an expert, with great images.

The image above is from a nice common-area garden between homes in Cardiff, CA, where some enterprising plant person decided to plant cuttings of various forms of jades – there are at least 5 different types shown here – and as you can see from the raised pipe, they did provide some irrigation. That is nice and will expedite growth, but once plants have reached a size as seen here, the water can be turned off and they will survive on their own.

At left is the typical and most common form of jade, the green, round-leaved *Crassula ovata* in full winter bloom. This plant is about 3 feet high, probably ten or more years old from a small plant.

At right is one of the forms of the hybrid known as *Crassula* 'Bluebird', a variable hybrid between *C. arborescens* and *C. ovata*.

Jades

Crassula ovata
'Hummel's Sunset'

Probably the most ubiquitous non-native succulent in California is the good old 'jade' plant, *Crassula ovata* (formerly *Crassula argentea*). It has been part of our landscape for well over a hundred years, will survive indefinitely in backyards and abandoned properties with no irrigation, shrinking in dry times and swelling out after rains. Jades abide. Transplants from the East Coast are sometimes surprised that their prized houseplant that they had nursed for years will grow like a weed out west. It is a very functional piece of green for any yard, but we take it for granted because it has been around so long and is so common. There are many newer forms, which you'll see on the following pages. They bloom with white to pinkish flower clusters in winter (there is a pink flower form as well). You can trim the lower branches to expose the trunk to make it look tree-like, or let it form large pillowy mounds. How do you propagate a jade? Break off a piece and throw it – it will root where it lands (as long as it lands on some dirt). Another common name for this crassula is the 'good luck' plant or 'money tree', which also applies to *Pachira aquatica*, among a few other plants. Please disregard these colloquial names in favor of the Latin, although 'jade' doesn't seem to have any competitors, so that one is cool.

There are many iterations of *Crassula ovata*, including the Toelken group discussed on the following pages. Above left is the small-leaved variety known as 'Crosby's Compact', 'Crosby's Dwarf', or sometimes as 'Crosby's Red' as it can blush red at times, named after horticulturist Harry Crosby. Above middle is a variegated form called 'Lemon-Lime' or 'tricolor', which can offer a two-tone contrast of a bright yellow with a darker green and a lighter yellow-green. Above right is the best white variegated form. Interestingly, when it reverts to green, as you can see on part of the plant here, it has a somewhat different leaf and stem structure than the classic round-leaved green form. At near left is the spectacular golden jade, usually called 'Hummel's Sunset' (named for hybridizer Ed Hummel). It can retreat to more green in shade or during wet winters, but usually keeps its bright yellow-gold in the sun, and can be a stunning plant in landscapes or in pots. Below left is an indeterminate variegated form, possibly the sunset variety in transition from green to gold. Below middle is the gloriously pink blooming form sometimes called 'Pink Beauty'. Out of flowering season, it is difficult to distinguish from the regular form of the common jade. Below right is an unusual variety with slightly undulated leaves and unique, spherical-shaped flower clusters. I acquired a piece of this plant many years ago via Paul Hutchinson of Tropic World nursery, and he called it 'wavy jade', which also might apply to *Crassula ovata v. undulata*, a quite distinct plant shown on page 199. In conclusion, there's a lot of jades.

Here is a trio of related but distinct cultivars of *Crassula ovata*. At left is the small-leaved form known as 'Crosby's Compact'. Top right is the traditional form, and the fluted-leaved plant in front is either *C. ovata* v. 'Hobbit' or 'Gollum' or 'Lady Fingers', depending on your interpretation. The state of flowers indicates that this image was taken in the winter months.

Right: a solid column of Golden Jade ('Hummel's Sunset').

Jades are incredibly resiliant growers in Southern California. The little rain-gutter squatter below is a piece that fell off a plant on a balcony above, rolled into the gutter, and found enough water and detritus to make a toehold.

'Hobbit' vs. 'Gollum' – the Toelken Jades

These wonderful permutations of *Crassula ovata* both make nice low-maintenance bonsai. They are different sports from the same original stock. The fanciful names are attributed to Helmut R. Toelken, who published a thesis on the revision of the crassulaceae in 1977. Although no relation to the J.R.R. Tolkien of Lord of the Rings renown, someone must have been inspired by the similar names to bestow these cultivars with their monikers. They are likely mutations that were culled in cultivation in the late 70s or early 80s, with the first reference to these names coming from Abbey Gardens and Grigsby's catalogs from that time. There is confusion as to which is which, plus there are several other distinguishable cultivars, known variously as 'Ladyfingers' and 'Dwarf Gollum', 'Ogre Ears', and 'E.T. Fingers', among a few others. I did encounter a large plant of the small leaved cultivar of *Crassula ovata* known as 'Crosby's Compact' (See page 194), that had several branches on one side mutate into what looks like 'Hobbit'. So that tells me that these mutations, which may be caused via mycoplasma (look it up), can appear spontaneously. As you can see from the plants below, both make fantastic bonsai subjects, only needing the proper small pot and some creative pruning. Leaves of both types can blush orange in cool winter conditions.

Thanks to Randy Baldwin for passing along an article by Roy Mottram in the July 2013 edition of *Crassulacea*, the journal of the International Crassulaceaen Network, (yes, that is a real thing – viva nerds!) that addresses this issue that has long been a bone of contention for me as a nurseryman and plant geek – except there is still so much confusion out there that I still don't know if I have them backwards here. I think Randy would say I have, based on his website, but I'm going with the way I learned it.

Crassula ovata 'Gollum', with its more gnarled trunk and exaggerated, folded, umbilicate leaves.

Crassula ovata 'Hobbit', usually has a smoother trunk, more uniformly cylindrical and tighter leaves with lens-shaped dimples on the tips. This is the more frequently encountered form.

Above left shows two Toelken mutations, the larger form of Gollum in front, with Hobbit behind. The middle photo shows Hobbit in full winter stress-induced orange coloration. Gollum doesn't seem to quite match that color. Top right is an excellent example of *C.* 'Gollum' in a bowl garden in Morro Bay, CA. Below left is a type of Gollum named 'E.T. Fingers'; there is another called 'Ogre Ears' (Shrek Ears?). They all look pretty similar. The middle photo is a variety that tends to grow lanky with smaller and more in-line leaves (v. 'Ladyfingers'?). The airy look seen here may also be partially due to container stress. Far right is a variegated form of Gollum.

Crassula arborescens, 'Silver Dollar Jade'

The white-purple color of this hardy jade makes an excellent landscape repetition plant, or works fine as a potted subject. Like most jades, it is slow-growing but easy to grow and propagate from cuttings. The species form has round leaves, as seen above left and below. There are several hybrids, the most prominent known as 'Blue Bird', seen above right. It has more ovate, slightly pointed leaves, and grows in a similar bushy manner, sometimes more floppy and white, others more compact and greenish as seen here. It is in fact a hybrid between *C. arborescens* and *C. ovata*. Both forms have white to pink small flower clusters from the winter into spring months.

Crassula arborescens ssp. undulatifolia (undulata)

This wonderful plant has been a happy surprise, popping into the market in the early 2000s, after being introduced via a Huntington ISI offering. It is a naturally occurring subspecies, not a selected cultivar or hybrid, and in my opinion is one of the best succulent introductions in a long time. It has wavy blue-green leaves, and grows into tight, compact and billowy bushes if left unchecked, or it can be trained into a nice bonsai. It grows easily from cuttings and is fairly temperature tolerant. There have been attempts to attach a few common names to this plant, including 'Blue Waves', 'Blue Curls', 'Ripple Jade', and 'Jitters'. It is a very reluctant bloomer, with typical winter white star cluster flowers when it gets around to it. The variation in leaf color and red edging in the plants below left are results of stress and conditions. The healthy growing color is a bluish-green as seen below right.

There are dozens of crassulas that grow with an appearance of leaves being stacked upon each other, with the stems coming right up the middle of the plant. The primary types are *Crassula perforata*, *Crassula rupestris*, and *Crassula capitella*, with a few crosses in between. There is a more extensive look at these on the Dave's Garden website, by Geoff Stein, with nice photos and more detail than I can go into in this book (although he cops to not being able to cover them all as well). Those in the rupestris complex have slightly thicker leaves and very ornamental, globeoid pinkish flowers. The perforata and capitella varieties have much longer, spindly flowers. As with most succulents, strong sunlight will keep them in a tight, compact form, until they begin to flower. In low-light conditions they will stretch and etiolate into an interesting, but not quite as eye-pleasing form.

Crassula capitella 'Baby Necklace'

There are a number of hybrids and cultivars of the stacked crassulas, but one of the best is seen at left, a hybrid called 'Baby Necklace', occasionally 'Watch Chain'. It maintains a tight, compact habit and burgundy coloration. It was created by legendary plantsman Myron Kimnach in the 1960s, a cross between *C. rupestris v. marnieriana* and *Crassula perforata*. A sport of that cross is called *C.* 'Baby's Surprise', with smaller, tighter rounded leaves seen at lower left corner in the image above.

Crassula perforata

This is likely the most common of the stacked crassulas. The primary form of the plant is a fairly large type, seen above. There is a more compact cultivar, below center, as well as several variegated forms, one of which is pictured below left. Don't confuse the species name 'perforata' with *Crassula perfoliata*, a species name that is associated with the common *C. perfoliata v. falcata* (usually referred to as just '*Crassula falcata*') on page 207.

Crassula rupestris

There are several delightful permutations of *Crassula rupestris*, both naturally occurring and cultivars. The red-edged form at left is known as 'High voltage'. There is green-and-teal blue form seen at middle right. The still colorful example above right may be closer to the true species, which you can see in a spirally growth form in habitat on Page 191.

Photo to left: Tina Zucker

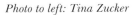

Left: *Crassula deceptor.*

Right: unidentifed, this one a possible cross of *Crassula pyramidalis*.

Above left: the very alien and biomechanical looking hybrid Crassula 'Buddah's Temple' is an established Myron Kimnach hybrid of the equally impressive *Crassula pyramidalis* with *Crassula perfoliata*. Above right is *Crassula capitella ssp. thyrsiflora ssp*. 'Red Pagoda' (large form) in its' highly (and temporarily) compact red stage. This plant is also sometimes called *Crassula corymbulosa* 'Shark's Tooth'. Some plants are blessed with too many names for their own good. Both images below are from the wonderful *C. falcata* cross known as 'Morgan's Beauty' or 'Morgan's Pink'. It is susceptible to brown 'rust' spots over time however.

Above left: A wonderful John Trager cross of *C. barkleyi* that at least visually improves on nature – the aptly named hybrid *Crassula* 'Pangolin'. Above middle: *Crassula columnella*. Above right: the minuscule *Crassula 'Caput minima'*. This is a different plant from the equally miniature form of *Crassula capitella* (minor).

Below left: a hybrid of *Crassula capitella*, similar to *C.* 'Red Pagoda', perhaps known as 'Purple Dragon'.

Below right: an excellent hanging plant, *Crassula pellucida (ssp. marginalis rubra)* is mostly seen in the variegated form shown here. I have this variegated form stress and shift into a deep red as well, so that may be where the 'rubra' (red) part of the name comes from. It also can be referred to as 'Calico Kitten' for some reason.

Crassula muscosa

I have mixed emotions about this prolific little succulent semi-weed. Pieces tend to crumble off and self-propagate, so beware where you plant it. There are quite a few forms, including a large form (above right), a dainty miniature form, a monstrose form (above left), a regular form, (background image), even a whitish variegated form (middle), and a crested form, which I used to have but sold it by mistake and can't find a picture of. It has very tiny chartreuse yellow flowers that have a distinct odor. The species name changed to the rather unpleasant name here, but was formerly known as *Crassula lycopoidioides*, which was one of my favorites to pronounce, which has an extra syllable hiding in there. The Latin 'muscosa' refers to 'moss', which the plant can look like from afar.

Crassula streyi

Crassula streyi is a gorgeous plant (left), with glossy green veined leaves with a deep burgundy underside. My experience is that it is not an easy grower, or we would see many more large specimens of this plant around. I think it is more of a greenhouse plant unfortunately.

Crassula tetragona

Sometimes referred to as the 'miniature pine tree' for its' somewhat bonsai feel (right), this long-established succulent is very easy to grow and propagate. Older specimens typically grow to several feet in height, but as the stem sheds the lower leaves, it can get a bit weedy and unkempt looking.

Crassula 'Campfire'

A splendidly hot colored and appropriately named form of *Crassula capitella, C.* 'Campfire' is a favorite for adding color pop to a landscape or dish garden. Like many plants that color up in reds or oranges, the color can be seasonal, accentuated by a healthy dose of sun and stress. There are times that it will be primarily green or yellowish green. In general it is a low, carpet-forming or cascading plant, but like most crassulas of this type, it will 'stand up' as it begins to flower, usually in fall or winter. The after-blooms will eventually brown and fade back, and the new growth will revert to compact and horizontal again.

Crassula falcata

Commonly known as the 'propeller plant', this is one of the more remarkable bloomers of the crassula genus. It reliably blooms around mid-summer – which is usually after most blooming succulents have finished flowering – with large clusters that look like red-orange broccoli. The more common form has blue-gray, flat and propellor-shaped leaves arranged geometrically. There are several other forms seen occasionally, such as the more lime-green version seen at right. Older plants can get leggy and unkempt looking, but can easily be clipped and started over. This plant has technically been reclassified as *Crassula perfoliata minor*, but nobody calls it that.

Photo: Karen Zimmerman

There are a few nice, dense, small-leaved and red blushing bushy crassulas. The pointed-leaved variety at left is *C. nudicaulis*, sometimes identified as *Crassula rubricaulis*. There is a beautiful new variegated form of this plant named 'Candy Cane' (below left), which unfortunately seems to be very prone to benign black spotting. The tiny-leaved form above middle is *Crassula pubescens v. radicans*. Above right is a similar looking, but larger-leaved variety known as *C. nudicaulis v. platyphylla*.

Below middle: a tall-growing hybrid of *Crassula mesembryanthimoides*. Below right: *Crassula pubescens v. radicans* in spring flower mode.

Crassula mesembryanthemoides

The species name is a mouthful, but it means it resembles some mesembs, which in fact it does. The real attraction of this plant is in the close-up view, as it is covered in fine white hairs, giving it an almost shimmering look. I've never seen it in a significantly large cluster to suggest use as a landscape plant, but it is an excellent container plant, either singly or in combination.

Crassula multicava

This lushly green and tropical-looking plant (below) is an excellent lower-story ground cover plant. It will happily grow in sunny locations, but its' best use is for lower-light, dappled shade locations, such as under a tree. In general, succulents aren't great under trees, due both to lower light and particularly because most don't look great covered in tree-leaf fallout. But a plant like this thrives in semi-shade, and often will absorb fallen leaves into the clump. It provides airy, pink-white flower from winter into spring.

Crassula pubescens

Below: Technically named *Crassula pubescens v. pubescens*, but who needs the redundancy. This little fuzzy guy qualifies as 'cute' by any definition of the word. It varies from burgundy/purple to green with red edges, and offers petite flowers as seen in inset below. It is rather microscopic, so plant accordingly.

Above left is the variegated form of *Portulacaria afra*, presented as bonsai. The plant above right is a tri-color variegated form also given the bonsai treatment. This variety may be named 'Roulant', or just 'Tricolor'. It seems to be more of a fussy grower than the rest of the group.

The most common form of *Portulacaria afra* is shown below, here resembling a habitat stand. This clump has been growing for years along Live Oak Road in Fallbrook, CA, without any irrigation. It will grow vertically and then begin to spread across the ground after a time. The plant on the facing page is equally ancient, but benefits from irrigation and some artistic bonsai-style trimming.

Portulacarias

These jade-like succulents really don't belong botanically in this crassula category at all. DNA analysis puts this genus much closer to the spiny didiereaceae group than to the crassulas, but they look so much like the latter -jades in particular – and are so often confused with them, that I'm sticking with the visually rather than botanically correct theme of this book and showing them here. Also known as 'elephant food' or 'elephant grass', *Portulacaria afra* is an indestructible plant in southern California (which also makes it very jade-like). Portulacarias bear no relation to portulacas, a small ground cover succulent, other than in the similarity of their names.

At left is an old *Portulcaria afra* trimmed into tree form – I want to call it bonsai but I think its too big to be a bonsai. This is a highly elastic and forgiving plant, and is an excellent candidate for bonsai, or given enough time, you can create a head-high hedge or fence.

Portulacaria afra variegata differs both in color and form from the vertical-growing green form. This bright yellow-leaved, red-stemmed plant generally begins as a prostrate growing, even cascading plant, but will eventually bunch up to a bush a few feet high – with usually an attendant skirt around the perimeter. It is a durable plant, great in a pot or landscape, with the same purple flower clusters as the green form in the summer months.

The plant below left has been planted in anticipation of cascading over and softening a wall-pocket garden, which it is beginning to do. The larger clump at right exhibits a vertical or climbing habit, with a four-foot high central column, supported somewhat by surrounding plants. In addition, it sends out lower branches to form a skirt.

Portulacaria afra in all forms flowers with delightful miniature lavender flower clusters, typically in mid-summer, as seen in the plant above (*P. afra minima* in this case).

Along with the two variegated forms seen on the facing and previous pages, a new type has recently appeared in cultivation, *P. afra* 'aurea', seen growing among echeverias below. The attraction with this plant is that it seems to intermingle pure yellow leaves with pure green, giving it a nice two-tone effect. The largest plant of this type that I've seen seems to grow both upright, and prostrate, with a ground cover skirt surrounding the central growth.

Portulacaria afra minima is an excellent cascading or ground cover succulent. It looks just like its upright growing sibling, but the emerald leaves are smaller (hence the name 'minima'), the stems are often redder, and it grows small and dense, only pushing up vertically a bit after a number of years. There appears to be one clone that remains prostrate, and another that will eventually push vertical in the middle, but as far as I can tell they are indistinguishable until the one starts to tent over time.

Order: Asterales
Family: Asteraceae
Genus: Senecio
Species: radicans

SENECIOS

Senecio vitalis (green)
and *Senecio mandraliscae* (blue)

An older name for this large group of daisy-related plants is 'compositae'. I've never heard anyone use the term 'compositae' in conversation, but the moniker refers to their similar composite flowers. In general, they are not spectacular flowering plants, but there are some exceptions. As you'll see on the following pages, the succulent members of this group (also including the genus othonna) can be very interesting plants, from tiny container creatures to cascaders, ground covers, or landscape bushes. There are also quite a few non-succulent senecios, which I'll leave to the proper authorities to described elsewhere.

Senecio jacobsenii

This is a great ground cover or cascading plant, with thick fleshy leaves that start green but will blush into a vibrant purple. It flowers infrequently with surprisingly bright orange flowers.

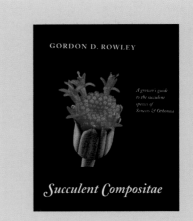

GORDON D. ROWLEY

A grower's guide to the succulent species & Othonna

Succulent Compositae

Succulent Compositae is, I believe, the only book dedicated to the succulent senecios (and the related and more obscure group othonna). I have to admit this might be my favorite cover image of any succulent book. Written by succulent authority Gordon D. Rowley, published by Strawberry Press in 1994, it is out of print but worth tracking down if you like these plants. It offers thorough information on all recognized species, with historical perspective – I only wish the images were a bit larger.

Senecio anteuphorbium

Senecio anteuphorbium is an upright, shrubby plant, with small green leaves aligned along green-gray stems. It flowers in fall with white puff-ball blooms, similar to many other senecios. The name refers to its reputed use as an antidote for euphorbia sap, although I can't find any conclusive evidence that it works. It does work as a nice, 3 to 4 foot high contrast plant against a plain wall, as seen here, and is a fairly rapid grower.

Senecio barbertonicus (below) will form a 3 to 4 foot diameter mound with yellow flowers of long duration in winter. It is easily grown from cuttings, and is ideally used as a background, softening or framing plant.

Senecio barbertonicus

When I first encountered this plant, I lumped it into the 'big, bushy green generic' type of plant. We succulent geeks tend to go for the sculptural and unique things. But not everything in a garden should be a 'wow, look at me' type of plant. There is a place for big, bushy green generic things. Soft and pillowy, sometimes from a distance these plants don't really at first look like succulents at all. Also in this category would be most jades. *Senecio barbertonicus* has long-lasting yellow winter flowers, and quite striking bright green foliage, and tends to keep its full shape for a long time. It is a nice mid-to-large addition to any garden, best planted towards the back as it can get large.

Photos: Tina Zucker

Senecio articulatus

Senecio articulatus

Commonly referred to as the 'Candle Plant' or the 'Hot Dog Cactus' (due to its periodic constrictions making it look like a chain of sausages), *Senecio articulatus* is an easy plant to grow and propagate. The more favored variegated form seen here offers bright purple and pink as well as white leaves to accompany the regular green. The color is usually stronger around the new-growth tips. Flowers are pale yellow, and it is fine with quite a bit of heat but doesn't want to freeze.

Senecio pendula

Appropriately named the 'Inchworm Plant', *Senecio pendula* has wonderful burgundy striated markings, and likes to grow wormlike and low to the ground. Flowers are a brilliant red. Look closely at the markings – they look like a stream of squid or jellyfish. Well, that's what I see.

As I put this book together, I realized that a number of the plants I'm covering here used to be more available ten or twenty or more years ago, but are now difficult to find, such as the *Senecio pendula* seen at right. There are a number of reasons for that, and I think the major one is that growers go where the demand is, and will always try to deal in plants that are fast or easy to propagate. And since there are so many new introductions now, some of the old favorites that might be a little slower or more laborious to propagate get put on the back burner. Some of the more rare plants are not only slow growers, but might be just difficult enough to grow and maintain that they have shifted more into the realm of the hobbyist or backyard grower. I'm always happy to see one of the larger growers bringing an old favorite back, which might just be a one-time impulse effort.

I mentioned earlier in the book that you'll see myriad cool and crazy plants on the internet, but quite a few of those are either impossible to find, very hard to grow, or photoshopped chimeras.

Senecio pendula

Senecio crassissimus

This senecio (left) somewhat resembles a silver dollar jade from afar, with a bit more green to the leaves, arranged in a linear manner along purple stems. The orange flowers are different from the jades, and it can reach four to five feet in height, sometimes getting rangy and gangly with age. However, it can easily be cut back into a fuller plant.

Senecio decaryi

A nice vertical growing shrub, *Senecio decaryi* (below) has silver-gray leaves with purple edges, seemingly arranged sideways on the stem at a 90 degree angle from the usual method of leaf attachment. It has small yellow – orange flowers, typical of the genus. This plant was erroneously introduced into cultivation as *Senecio amaniensis*, which has a similar leaf structure, but entirely differerent, orange pendulous flowers, seen left.

Senecio decaryi

Photo: Randy Baldwin

Senecio amaniensis

This shrubby plant (bottom left) forms a considerable mound in the garden, with large green leaves and nice orange pendulous flowers encased in a dusky purple bell.

Senecio haworthioides

Right: This must be the most strikingly white succulent, exclusive of some of the dudleyas. Not really a durable landscape plant, it is best kept contained, and seems to like warm conditions. It can rot in too much wet and cold, and like many succulents, older specimens can get more leggy and woody than the perfect little clump seen here.

Senecio kleiniformis

Below: *Senecio kleiniformis* has soft and very blue tricorn leaves, and is sometimes referred to as the 'Spearhead ' plant. It is an excellent container plant, and will cascade a bit.

Senecio vitalis

Also known as *Senecio talinoides*, this plant resembles the smaller blue chalk sticks in leaf shape, but is more of a green to aqua-green, and much more of an upright and mounding plant. It is very easy to grow, and is an excellent landscape plant, but bear in mind that it is a fairly large and aggressive grower, and perhaps should be kept in back. It will overtake all the other plants in a container garden. It does provide a nice softness for a repetition plant in a succulent landscape. There is a nice crested form as well.

Senecio serpens

Senecio ficoides

There are two distinctive blue senecios popular today, the smaller and slower-growing *S. serpens*, seen above, and the larger growing *S. mandraliscae*, seen below. There is another less available blue senecio, *Senecio ficoides* (inset) with larger and more flattened blue leaves. *Senecio serpens* (sometimes called 'repens') is better in small spaces, grows more compact and less floppy than the larger forms, and might be a bit more of an intense blue in season. Like *S. mandraliscae*, it is also somewhat of a cascading succulent (see page 222) for the right situation. All of these plants take on a more gray-greenish blue color in the summer heat, returning to peak color in the cool winter months. *S. mandraliscae* is preferred for larger areas as it is a much faster grower, but can get floppy and overtake smaller plants. Flowers are typical of most senecios, unremarkable white puff balls on short stems.

Senecio mandraliscae

Senecio radicans

Above and right: two distinct forms of the cascading *Senecio radicans*. The light green, more compact form is sometimes called the 'String of Bananas', also shown above. The more blue form is 'Fishhook'. They look good growing together. On the far right edge of the image at right there is also a cascading string of *Senecio serpens*, not usually thought of as a cascader, but it will once it reaches the edge of the pot.

Senecio macroglossus

I put this variegated, waxy leaved 'ivy' vine in the 'that's a succulent?' category. In fact you might be more likely to find

one in the house plant section of your nursery, but it is indeed a thick and fleshy leaved climber, very succulent and sun-loving in nature.

Senecio radicans

Known as the 'string of bananas' or 'fishhook' senecio, there appears to be two distinct forms of this plant, both answering to the same common names. Both are excellent cascading plants for hanging pots. The inset above is much more blue with larger, more spaced apart and upright/erect leaves. There is a species called *Senecio abbreviatus* that resembles this second form, but that name is rarely encountered in the trade.

Senecio herreianus

I have to stifle a giggle when I say this plant name out loud. Sorry, I need to grow up, but say it our loud and tell me you're not amused. This less-frequently encountered 'string' senecio differs from *S. rowleyanus* with its slightly larger and more football-shaped 'leaves', which usually exhibit subtle striping as well. It also can color-shift from green at times to more of a pink color.

Senecio rowleyanus

Always a favorite, this is one of the best of the cascading suc-culents. Commonly known as the 'String of Pearls' ('String of Peas' would be a more apt description), it sports dainty white-purple flowers that smell like clove. It has a tendency to burn in too much sun, but this usually happens more to a plant that hasn't had time to acclimate to direct sun. I have seen quite a few healthy exam-

ples growing in full (albeit coastal) sun. It does seem to grow best in partial or limited sun, and will respond to frequent watering and fertilizing. There is a less seen variegated form with light pinkish, pearlescent leaves, which might be the more accurate form for the common name.

Senecio oxyriifolius ssp. tropaeolifolius (mini)

The form seen here (left) is apparently the miniature form of the larger type species, which does have a significantly different and less cupped leaf. Its growth habit is most accurately described as a 'scrambler', serving as either a smallish ground cover or cascader. There are some plants that I can just never remember the name of, and then I look up the name – like this one (c'mon!) – and don't feel so bad. I usually prefer Latin over common names, but you can make exceptions – although I don't think this one has a common name.

Senecio kleinia

This plant may have been reclassified as *Kleinia nerifolia*, but is still mostly known as a large-form senecio. It is a Canary Islands endemic, indeed mimicking its much larger Canaries native, *Dracaena draco*, also known as the Dragon Tree. *Senecio kleinia* can grow into an 6 foot tall mini-tree over time. It has thick, sausage-like green stems. Like most Canary Island plants, it goes through a period of summer dormancy, leafing out again after the first fall rains. Flowers are typically non-descript, puffy white like most senecios (or kleinias).

Senecio medley-woodii

Senecio medley-woodii is an attractive bushy succulent with fuzzy white-gray leaves and mild leaf serrations. It has bright yellow and orange daisy-type flowers in the warmer months, and is typically evergreen in nature. The purple-flowered plant below may or may not be properly named; it is distinct but information on it is scant at present.

Senecio leandrii

*Senecio
scaposus*

The species form of this white-coated plant has the 'fingery' appearance of the plant inset right, very much resembling one of the finger-leaved dudleyas. A more interesting variety is *S. scaposis v. addoensis*, shown in the large background photo and inset left, and borrowing John Trager's description, looks like the leaf tips were flattened and crimped like the edge of a pie crust (i.e. 'spathulate'). These are best treated as container plants, and have showy yellow flowers. It does seem to prefer being on the dry side in the hot summer months, so resist watering even if it seems thirsty.

Senecio stapeliaeformis

Left: The name *Senecio stapeliaeformis* is a nod to the stapeliad-like shape of the 'leaves', which also have attractive dusky purple-on-green patterning. It has a bright red flower.

Senecio pyramidatus

Right: *Senecio pyradmidatus* forms a multi-head bush, usually very full in nature with yellow daisy flowers. It is reputed to be very drought-tolerant.

Order: Saxifragales
Family: Crassulaceae
Genus: Sedum
Species: rubrotinctum

*Sedum
rupestre*

SEDUMS

lso known by their old informal name of 'stonecrop', many if not most sedums qualify as succulents, but a number of them prefer cooler and wetter climates and do not tolerate heat, particularly those native to northern Europe. Still others tend to die back after blooming, or just don't quite fit into the 'succulent' category, such as the popular *Sedum* 'Autumn Joy'. For our purposes here we will focus on the warm-weather succulent sedums, which as a whole are low-lying, mat-forming small leaved plants. Some are fairly dainty, and despite being succulents they might require more water and a bit less sun. Others are long established players in the ornamental succulent category. They can make nice accent plants in dish gardens, and quite a few are excellent cascading plants.

Sedum spathulatum

Sedum 'Dragon's Blood'

Sedum hispanicum

The sedums on this page are the type of tiny carpet-like plants that many people think of when you're talking about sedums. Most are generally happy in mediterranean climates, but some are heat sensitive and can approach being more like alpine plants. They can be quick to show the need for water in hot weather, particular the chartreuse form known as *Sedum* 'Gold Moss' (*S. acre 'aureum'*), seen middle row right.

Sedum angelina

Sedum acre 'aureum'

Unidentified

Sedum confusum

Sedum rubrotinctum

Commonly called 'Pork and Beans' or maybe more appropriately 'Jellybeans', this lovely little clumper/cascader ranges from apple green to reddish to orange depending on season and conditions, with clusters of yellow flowers in the spring. There is a pink form called either 'aurea' or 'Aurora', inset above. It is an excellent companion plant for dish gardens, although it is brittle and easily breaks apart when handled.

Sedum cauticola 'lidakense'

All of the dainty, carpet forming sedums on this page are better suited to dish garden conditions rather than more difficult inground applications. There are several other blue and blue-gray sedums that are quite similar.

Sedum hernamdezii is one of several small 'jellybean' sedums. It is a dainty, bright emerald-green plant, great for dish gardens or small rockeries as seen here. It has yellow star-shaped flowers, and is closely related to *Sedum furfuraceum*.

Sedum dasyphyllum minor

Sedum rupestre 'Blue Spruce'

Sedum hintonii right, is a delicate plant with miniature hair-like filaments. This example may be variegated, as it has a much lighter skin color than the typical green.

Sedum hintonii

Sedum stahlii

Left is *Sedum stahlii*, also known as 'Coral Beads' or 'Mexican Sedum' (although there are quite a few sedums from Mexico). It is a small ground cover type plant, which can range from dark green to red as seen here. It is very delicate to the touch, but the detached 'beads' can form new plants. It blooms with tiny yellow star-shaped flowers.

Sedum clavatum

This is an excellent dish garden or landscape plant. It forms a tight blue or blue-gray clump, and will cascade. It has nice white flower clusters as seen at right, and will blush pinkish in the summer months. I've always had a difficult time remembering that this is a sedum, as it looks like a pachyveria or graptopetalum cross. It is considered to be in a category of 'pachysedums', which are not in fact man-made crosses, but are a handful of species sedums with fat leaves as exhibited here.

Sedum morganianum

This is one of the better known of the cascading succulents. There are at least two primary leaf forms, one with rounder and smaller leaves – usually called *Sedum* 'Burrito' (photo below). The longer/larger and more downward-pointing leaved variety is apparently the true species, properly called just *Sedum morganianum* (at right). And to further confuse things, both are often referred to as 'Donkey's Tail' or 'Burro's Tail' (which might be where 'burrito' came from). Apparently *S.* 'Burrito' is a vegetative sport of the primary plant. Color can vary from lime green to more of a blue-green, with infrequent burgundy flowers at the end of the growing tips. Although it is generally an easy plant to grow, they are brittle and difficult to move without breaking, and wind or birds can cause stems to strip. To grow full plants like the two old-timers seen here, you need a nice protected environment, and a fairly large pot to allow for such luxuriant growth.

Sedum furfuraceum

There are several tree sedums from Mexico, and one of the best for bonsai is *Sedum frutescens*. It can be deciduous in winter, and is at times a temperamental grower, probably better as a container plant. The visually similar relative is *Sedum oxypetalum*, with a similar tree shape and rounder leaves. Another rarely seen and more difficult grower is *S. torulosum*.

Sometimes referred to as the 'bonsai' sedum for its bonsai potential and just natural appearance, *Sedum furfuraceum* is a cold-tolerant small ground cover or crevice dweller from high elevations in Mexico. Never reaching much size, it can be an interesting companion plant in a dish garden or for accents in an outdoor rockery. It has small white star-shaped flowers, and can be propagated by cuttings.

Sedum frutescens

Sedum multiceps

Also known as the 'Pygmy Joshua Tree' for obvious reasons, this little beauty (left) is a favorite of those that enjoy bonsai succulents. Unfortunately this winter grower doesn't like the summer months, and it tends to collapse in warm weather. The plant at left will usually wilt and lay down in the heat; it might survive and regain its former shape the next fall, or it might not.

Sedum prealtum /
Sedum dendroideum

It is difficult to tell the difference between these two 'tree' sedums. They actually grow more bushy, to around a 2 to 3 foot diameter. Reportedly cold and draught tolerant, they feature apple-green rosette leaves, that can blush red at times, with yellow flower clusters in winter and spring. Similar to many aeoniums, they can look full for a few years, but older plants tend to get leggy or a bit beat-up looking, and might need to be cut back, thinned or replaced (the latter would be easy by just cutting and re-rooting the heads).

Sedum nussbaumerianum/Sedum adolphi

This, or these, are great plants for swaths of succulent color. The fat leaf arrangement makes them easy to confuse with a pachyphytum or graptopetalum, but the flowers will tell you otherwise. There is confusion over the names, and while this isn't definitive, I believe the fat-leaved plant above right is *Sedum nussbaumerianum*, while the thinner-leaved plant above with darker edge stripes is *S. adolphi* (sometimes referred to as 'Firestorm'). In fact the name 'nussbaumerianum' may soon be retired altogether, which would be a shame as it is one of my favorite plant names. You will also see common name such as 'Coppertone' or 'Golden Sedum' or 'Golden Glow' applied to one or both. The color can vary depending on conditions and time of year, from a golden yellow/gold to at times a spotted, rusty tint, or even become lime-green for a time. It has nice clustering white flowers, and is easy to propagate. As you can see on the facing page, it can provide excellent garden color when mass-planted.

Order: Saxifragales
Family: Crassulaceae
Genus: Kalanchoe
Species: beharensis

KALANCHOES

Kalanchoe fedschenkoi

Photo: John Trager

A subdued, dusky color contrast of *Kalanchoe fedtschenkoi* with an aenomium provides a soft and subtropical feel as lower-story landscape plants.

Below left: *Kalanchoe tomentosa* 'Chocolate Soldier' and *K. eriophylla*, a couple of cute fuzzies. Below middle: *Kalanchoe bracteata* 'Silver Spoons'. Below right: a new clutivar of *Kalanchoe tomentosa* named 'Teddy Bear' displays more compact and paw-shaped leaves, a bit distinct from the longer-leaved brown 'Chocolate Soldier'.

Kalanchoes are tropical to subtropical succulents from Madagascar and Eastern Africa. Not exactly desert dwellers, most originate in the transition zones between deserts and higher rainfall regions. Many handle somewhat cool and wet winter temperatures, making them fairly easy in cultivation. The genus is properly pronounced 'kal-un-KO-ee' or 'kal-un-KO-uh', although it is often pronounced the way it looks like it should be if you read it phonetically, 'kal-ANCH-oh'. The most well-known kalanchoes are the various cultivars of *K. blossfeldiana*. They graduate from the hothouse in glorious bloom, but I've seldom had one bloom again quite as robustly as the plant I first purchased, and you rarely encounter long-enduring examples of *K. blossfeldiana* in the landscape.

You will see the genus name 'bryophyllum' sometimes associated with some kalanchoes. That dates back to a few naming issues from the 1800s, but the entire genus is generally referred to in the trade as 'kalanchoe'. However, some botanists will use 'bryophyllum' in association with many of the 'mother of millions' plants (Page 255). These multipliers all have downward-facing bell shaped flowers, which is supposed to be the indicators of the 'bryophyllum types'. But few people use that term. They're kalanchoes.

There are a number of hairy or fuzzy kalanchoes, and others that form nice green pillowy bushes, often with bell-shaped flowers in winter or spring. Kalanchoes like a temperate climate and do not react well to a freeze.

Kalanchoe blossfeldiana

Above is a perfect-looking example of *Kalanchoe luciae*, showing a propensity for undulating leaves. At right are some examples of the plant that grow more vertical, up to two feet high. Normally this is an example of the plant beginning to elongate into a flower like the one on the facing page, but this particular clone just grew this way (only to later continue to elongate into a bloom as they all do). Below is an example of what often happens: a clump will look good for a number of years, but after a while it can get scraggly for unknown reasons. In this case, there had been a few blooming events over the years, resulting in a denser population, but after a while it just began to go downhill. One thing I've learned, the plant loves sun and heat, and in those conditions it also is happy with quite a bit of water, so try to plant in full sun with a good depression or trough around the plant to collect water; providing it can still drain.

Kalanchoe luciae

Commonly called the 'Paddle Plant' or 'Flapjacks', *Kalanchoe luciae* (formerly known also as *K. thyrsiflora*, which is actually a close relative with less of the red coloring, shown on the following page) is one of the most popular succulents in cultivation. It can form compact, deep red to orange-red clusters. There is some variability wherein certain strains may grow taller and with more undulations. There is also a variegated form seen at right and on page 8 known as 'Fantastic'. *K. luciae* exhibits a monocarpic flowering event as seen below, where the rosette itself elongates into a tall, fuzzy white flower spire. The stalk will eventually go brown and wither away and can be removed, but like many plants, the dying part triggers new growth below, so after a time of ugliness, you will end up with more plants and a fuller clump.

Kalanchoe thyrsiflora

This was the erroneous species name attributed to *K. luciae* until the early 2000s. *Kalanchoe thyrsiflora* (sometimes misspelled or mispronounced 'thrysiflora') is a closely related form with similar fleshy, paddle-like leaves. It doesn't blush red like *K. luciae*, but has an attractive powdery white-green leaf, usually arranged in a more symmetrical fashion. It also has a more impressive (and scented) terminal flower. This species has almost become extinct in cultivation since the advent of the more colorful *K. luciae*, but it shouldn't be, as it is an excellent ornamental succulent.

Kalanchoe fedtschenkoi

This is a fantastic plant for containers or landscape. The primary type is a dull glaucous/green, but the variegated form shown below is the most popular. Copious pink winter flowers can give a large drift a month-long resemblance to a soft pink wave, as seen at left.

Pastel-pink flowers of a swath of *Kalanchoe fedtschenkoi* add soft color contrast to the blue *Senecio serpens* and *Agave americana*. This image was taken in January at the entrance to the marvelous Lotusland botanical garden near Santa Barbara, CA.

Kalanchoe marnieriana

Very similar in appearance to *K. fedtschenkoi* and *K. rotundifolia*, *Kalanchoe marnieriana* is a more compact bush with gray-green leaves that can blush with pink edging in winter or spring. It has delicate clusters of pinkish bell-shaped flowers in the winter months, and is reputed to be more shade-tolerant than many of its' relatives.

Kalanchoe rotundifolia

K. rotundifolia is very attractive with round, symmetrically arranged leaves. It can lose some charm as it grows, but has nice red flowers. As mentioned above, it looks an awful lot like *K. marnieriana*, and differs from *K. fedtschenkoi* primarily by its more compact growing habit.

Kalanchoe pumila

This distinct little plant (left) has nice white-gray and slightly fuzzy, scalloped-edged leaves. Older leaves fade a bit, giving it a two-tone effect, and it can grow into a tight little clump, cascading if allowed to grow over an edge. This makes it a nice hanging pot plant. It also has very attractive lavender pink flowers in spring.

Kalanchoe eriophylla

A bit harder to find than the other 'panda plants' (*Kalanchoe tomentosa*), this related species (above) is sometimes called the 'Snow White Panda Plant', the 'Blue Kalanchoe' (as it is supposed to be blue under all the white hairs), or the 'Snow Bunny'. It has lavender pink flowers, very similar to *K. pumila*, which indicates that it might be more closely related to that plant. This plant deserves more popularity

Kalanchoe millotii

K. millotii (left) qualifies as a cute little teddy bear of a plant. Slightly fuzzy, silver-green leaves have scalloped edges, and it blooms with pink flowers emerging from fuzzy bracts. It stays farily small, and can get somewhat rambly in the landscape, but is excellent as a container plant.

Above left: *Kalanchoe beharensis v.* 'Oakleaf'. Above middle: *K. beharensis* 'minima'. Above right: a slightly rounder-leaved iteration of K. 'Oakleaf'.

Background: *Kalanchoe beharensis* 'Fang' with its characteristic leaf back 'fangs'. Left: *K. beharensis subnudum* grows to the same size as the fuzzy 'type' species, but has smooth, light green leaves.

One of the more unique and noteworthy of the larger soft succulents is *Kalanchoe beharensis*, one of the 'felt plants', sometimes called the the 'Velvet Elephant Ear' or 'Napoleon's Hat'. The latter is actually not a good comparison at all, as the leaves much more resemble the tricorn hats from the 1800s. The most common form can grow to over ten feet in height, with multiple branches. Like a few of the other brown felt kalanchoes, it offers a two-tone brown leaf arrangement, with the new leaves exhibiting a rich golden velvet brown, particularly on the upper portion of the leaves, while the bottom sides and lower leaves fade to a lighter brown. Old leaves will shrivel and fall, leaving a trunk with a geometric series of divots where the leaf stems calved off, which can be quite sharp to the touch. The trunk of this plant might be the only succulent in this book to have caused me to bleed. The inflorescence is large, branched, fuzzy and rather unremarkable, seen below. There are a few nice cultivars, including the 'Brown Dwarf' (minima), 'Oakleaf', 'Fang', and the smooth green hairless form known as *v. subnuda* or *nudum*, all of which are featured on the facing page. These kalanchoes are subtropical Madagascan plants and are very tender to any hint of frost.

Kalanchoe beharensis

Kalanchoe orgyalis

This two-tone beauty grows into a small shrub, up to several feet high and across. Sometimes called the 'pottery plant', likely due to its terra cotta coloring, or 'Copper Spoons', it exhibits a golden cinnamon color on the upper side of its felty leaves, with a more brown-gray underside to the leaf. The upper sides will eventually fade to the same color as the bottom as the leaf ages, but new growth always provides the richer color. It flowers with yellow flowers in the spring. Generally pronounced with a hard 'g', some folks get a kick out of the name, which is actually derived from a Greek word describing the plant's size.

The species name 'tomentosa' translates to 'hairy', which applies to several other kalanchoes but has found a home with this little beauty, also called the 'panda plant' due to its fuzzy hugginess. The primary white type with brown leaf-edge spots is seen at right. It can become a small-to-mid sized plant, perhaps a foot or two in diameter, after a few years. There is a brown variety, below right, called the 'chocolate panda' or sometimes the 'chocolate soldier'. Another less-seen cultivar is the larger-leaved white variety seen left below, which has attractive bright golden brown markings on the newer leaf edges, which fade over time to a darker color, giving it a two-tone appearance. There are some rare cultivars, such as 'Super Fuzzy' and 'Golden Girl', and more that are in the realm of collector plants. Like the other velvety kalanchoes, flower stalks are also fuzzy, with small burgundy flowers opening at the tips of the stalks, best appreciated up close (center image). Care and propagation is easy, as a new plant will sprout from a leaf base.

Kalanchoe tomentosa

Top left: the miniature *Kalanchoe rhombopilosa*, a little container curiosity. Middle Right: This plant has to be *Kalanchoe laetivirens* because the tag at the Huntington Botanic Garden says so. The plant at top right is unidentified, but has a similar flower and is likely the same. The winter dusky rose flower stalks are tall and relatively long-lasting.

Above and at left in flower is a recently introduced compact kalanchoe, *K. laxiflorus ssp. violacea.*

Kalanchoe marmorata

Also known by the colloquial name 'the Pen-Wipe Plant' the Latin in this name ('marmorata') refers to the spotted leaves. There are cultivars of the same plant with almost no spots, seen below left. The spotless form usually exhibits extra large leaves as well. Most forms of *K. marmorata* form a nice full bush, a few feet across and high, with impressive, large white star shaped flowers in winter through spring.

A 'Mother of Millions' kalanchoe sending new plantlets down the assembly line.

Kalanchoe daigremontiana 'Parsel Tongue'

Photo: John Trager

Kalanchoe gastonis-bonnieri is a nice and somewhat exotic-looking creature that will develop little plantlets at the leaf tips only, as seen at top – more like a 'mother of a couple at a time'. It nevertheless follows the same asexual reproduction as the other plants seen on these pages, and is an excellent hanging basket candidate.

Bottom right is *Kalanchoe (Bryophyllum) tubiflora*, one of the most aggressive, or prolific if you prefer, of the 'mother of millions' kalanchoes. Plantlets from leaf tips have invaded the pot of aloe vera and are threatening to choke it out. The at one time solitary aloe might eventually lose the battle to the invading hoard of newcomers. If it weren't so invasive, I'd recommend the plant, as it has a nicely patterned leaf and pretty red bell flowers in winter. But once you have one, you'll never get red of them. Consider yourself warned.

Kalanchoe daigremontiana

'Mothers of Millions' kalanchoes

'Mother of hundreds,' or maybe thousands, would be a more accurate moniker for these prolific succulents, but 'millions' is better alliteration and it sure seems like millions of baby plants take root with zero outside help. Take the *Kalanchoe diagremontiana (Kalanchoe laetivirens?)* at left. Try counting all the little baby plants lined up on the leaf edges. Every one will likely fall off and begin to grow. I don't know if anyone has ever even tried to grow one from seed – why would you? Perhaps to make a hybrid? Some do in fact have nice bell-shaped flowers, typically in the winter months. I hesitate to call them 'invasive', as they will only colonize the area directly below the parent plant. But if you have other container plants in the shadow of one of these kalanchoes, well, read about the pot of plants on the bottom left of the facing page. Technically, these are considered to be the representatives of the genus bryophyllum, but that term is seldom used.

The neon pink plant below is a hybrid called *K.* 'Pink Butterflies'. Although it does form leaf-edge plantlets, the variegation inhibits chlorophyl, making them too weak to form roots once they fall. The one 'mother of millions' I wish would reproduce won't do it.

Kalanchoe 'Pink Butterflies'

There are at least several climbing kalanchoes, two of which are featured here. At right is the dark-foliaged *K. beauverdii*, and at left is an at first unidentified form given to me by my friend Arnie after a trip to Madagascar. A piece somehow hitched a ride in his suitcase. He said it isn't rare over there, almost a weed, and the little piece he gave me is starting to climb all over my plant collection. I found out it is *Kalanchoe schizophylla*, introduced by the ISI a few years back. It is an aggressive grower, but is just weird enough to be endearing – very much a plant for a science fiction movie backdrop.

Kalanchoe beauverdii

Below left is *Kalanchoe sexangularis* ('six-edged leaves'), which has seasonally deep red leaves and yellow flowers. Below right is *Kalanchoe humilis*, more of a container-miniature collector specimen plant.

Kalanchoe carnea 'Modoc'

This is an excellent foliage succulent, growing up to five feet high with large leaves. It has a tropical look, but will tolerate minimal irrigation. However, it is a plant that will take water whenever it can get it, and will grow large and fast with irrigation. Its' thick succulent stems are very similar to *Kalanchoe prolifera*. It is a long-established plant in California, easily grown from cuttings and will tolerate full sun along the coast, preferring afternoon shade from the inland heat. Another name for *Kalanchoe carnea* may be *K. petitiana*.

Below left: Also known as 'Jurassic Kale' or the 'Jack and the Beanstalk' plant for its rapid growth rate, this plant, like the tropical-looking 'Modoc', can do without too much water, but if you indulge it, it will take off on you, from one foot to 6 foot plus in less than a year. It elongates into large bell flowers, with clusters of baby plantlets forming along the leaf nodes (below far

Kalanchoe streptanthus

right), dropping and rooting much like the 'mother of millions' types. You can keep it constricted and stressed into a nice bonsai in a pot if you prefer.

Kalanchoe prolifera

Kalanchoe hybrids

Most kalanchoes in cultivation are true species, although some are polymorphic and differ from the primary type. They also are candidates for hybridization, and there are some nice crosses being worked on, such as the the plant at left. There are not enough, to my knowlededge, in cultivation yet to offer any particular hybrid names to search for, but that should change. *K. blossfeldiana* in particular is being crossed for impressive flowers.

The *Kalanchoe suarezensis* plants I photographed at bottom left at the Huntington Botanical Garden might be the only examples of this species I've seen. Large winter flowers look like red inflated seed pods. An even more impressive bloom belongs to *K. mortagei*, a similarly long-leaved plant with even more impressive large red/orange flowers. Unfortunately it is also rare in cultivation, and a plant I only know at present from the internet.

Kalanchoe synsepala

The hanging plant at left comes in several forms. The large-leaved type is seen at left. A tighter, red edged form is shown below. It is sometimes called the 'walking kalanchoe', as it sends out long shoots with new plantlets at the tips, which will cascade down from a hanging pot, giving it the appearance of a creature supported by thin legs.

Kalanchoe suarezensis

Kalanchoe bracteata

Kalanchoe bracteata 'Silver Spoons' (above) is a silver-white pubescent bushy plant, almost identical to another species named *K. hildebrandtii*, differing primarily in flower color. *K. bracteata* has red flowers, as seen in inset, and *K. hildebrandtii* has more of a yellow-white bloom. Side by side you can see a slight difference in leaf formation, but they are very similar. There is a green form as well, seen at left, which also has an upright habit.

Conditions can alter a plant's appearance somewhat. The sort of evenly-spaced, semi-cartoonish growth in large image above are on plants that are in quite a bit of shade. The plant in inset is in more full sun, the leaves are more compact, and the lower leaves have even shed some hair, creating a brown contrast to the mostly white plant. The brown leaves make it look quite a bit like its close relative *K. orgyalis*.

Order: Saxifragales
Family: Crassulaceae
Genus: Cotyledon
Species: orbiculata

Most people pronounce this genus name as 'Kaht-uh-LEE-dun', although you will occasionally hear it as 'Kah-TILL-uh-dawn' (like a dinosaur name).

Cotyledons are generally soft-leaved, shrubby succulents, some with very white, powdery leaves. They are mostly mid-size plants that are excellent in the landscape, although some can get woody and unkempt after a number of years. Most have attractive, pendulous bell flowers on tall stalks in the winter to spring months. Most cotyledons in cultivation are from Africa and do well in mediterranean climates.

If you google 'cotyledon', usually the first thing that shows up for that word is an entirely different subject. The same word refers to the the first embryonic leaf of a seed-bearing plant, which will sound familiar to anyone that has studied Botany 101.

In cultivation, nearly all of the various forms of cotyledon available are all subspecies or regional forms (and now hybrids of) *Cotyledon orbiculata*. There are several forms with attractive undulating leaves, which used to be divided into the species *C. undulata*, but now are all subsumed into *C. orbiculata (f. undulata)*.

The three varieties shown on this page are all varying forms of *Cotyledon orbiculata*. The plant below left is an African habitat image by Jeremy Spath.

Above left: there are several tubular-leaved varieties of *C. orbiculata*. Most are tagged as *C. orbiculata v. oblanga* or *flaniganii*. There are also cultivar names such as 'Happy Dancing Girl', v. 'Flavida', 'Lady Fingers, etc. I'm not sure there is much consensus on which is which. Above right is a very white form, perhaps *v. dinteri*. Below right is a new cultivar called 'Mint Truffels'. Notice the resemblance to *Kalanchoe synsepala* on page 258. There is a bit of convergent evolution in the succulent world. Below left is the very attractive cultivar known as 'Elk horn'. The elk horn shape doesn't seem to be stable, as I've seen some revert to more cylindrical leaves at times.

Cotyledon macrantha

The technically correct name for this plant is *Cotyledon orbiculata v. oblonga macrantha*, but who wants to say all that? I've always called it the big green cotyledon. It has attractive, large red/orange hanging bell flower clusters from winter into spring, and is very durable and long established in California. Like many succulents, it is very drought tolerant, but will look full and lush if watered more. It can form a fairly good-sized clump, almost a hedge over time, and is easy to grow from cuttings. Perhaps not a feature specimen plant, it can be an excellent background framing element in a succulent garden, in the same vein as how many large jades can function.

The precious 'Bear Paws' plant, *Cotyledon ladismithensis*. The attractive variegated form is shown here. There is a similar species called *Cotyledont tomentosa*.

Cotyledon ladismithensis

Above left: a tubular leaved form of *Cotyledon orbiculata*, sometimes called 'Ladyfingers', exhibiting seasonal purple tips. Above center is one of the finest forms of *f. undulata*. Far right image is the more rare *Cotyledon sinus-alexandrii*. It forms a dense little mound of tightly packed, balloon-like green 'leaves', and is summer dormant, shedding all leaves and looking sort of dead. It will wake up in spring with very nice purple-white flowers, followed by new leaves.

Below are two nice white-foliaged forms of *Cotyledon orbiculata*. The plant on the left is probably the whitest iteration, and the plant on the right is one of several that exhibit nice burgundy leaf edging.

Tylecodons

A closely related group are the tylecodons, which are a bit more on the slow-growing, collector side of the hobby, and can make nice container or bonsai plants. The word 'tylecodon' is an anagram of cotyledon, and these plants were spun off from that related genus some time ago. They behave quite differently, primarily in the tylecodons being winter-growing, summer deciduous plants.

By contrast, cotyledons are usually evergreen, maintaining leaves year-round. Tylecodons usually begin to flower as the leaves fall in late spring. They can be quite stunning sculptural plants, many offering a bonsai appeal. The most common is *Tylecodon paniculata*, above. At left are smooth-trunked hybrids of *T. wallichii*, which has similar leaves in the true species form, but with a knobby or spiky trunk structure.

Tylecodon wallichii

'Baby's Toes' *(Fenestraria aurantiaca)*, above, is a favorite of almost anyone that has seen it. The surprisingly large white or yellow daisy-style flowers are a nice surprise. At right is another ground cover/cascader, *Oscularia deltoides*, with nice little pink flowers in spring. Below are two forms of the 'Tiger Jaws', *Facuaria tigrina*. They might look ferocious, but are completely soft like all mesembs. It flowers with nice orange or orange-yellow flowers in the fall.

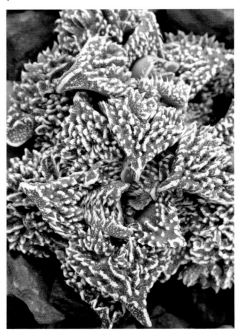

MESEMBS

esembryanthemums represent a huge group of soft and succulent plants, primarily from southern Africa. Based on the size and diversity of the group, they probably deserve a much larger portion of this book than do the echeverias and aeoniums, but are not quite as ubiquitous in the trade as the other succulents herein. Some are fantastic ground cover plants, such as the various types of lampranthus ('ice plants') as seen above. Others are dainty little container creatures. Many mimic rocks, belying their true identity when in flower. You can't get much more succulent than these soft, plump little bundles of juice.

Mesembs generally are not rosette shaped like many of the succulents in this book, and thus sometimes have more of an alien-creature appeal, which works for some folks and not so much with others. Most reside under the family aizoaceae, with many but not all falling in the genus mesembryanthemum. So the broad term 'mesemb' isn't botanically accurate for all plants considered 'mesembs', but it has become the default term for a whole host of plants that just look like . . . mesembs.

Cheriodopsis candidissima, blushing purple in the winter cold.

Above left: *Fenestraria auriantaca* next to a gibbaeum. Above right: a tight clump of lithops, also know as living rocks. These can be among the most difficult of succulents to grow, very susceptible to overwatering. If you can figure out how to keep them happy, they are incredibly cool plants, but are among the most often-killed of all succulents. At left is an example of a cheiridopsis. Early winter flowers can last up to several weeks. Below left is a type of argyroderma (ot possibly a gibbaeum) – a lithops-like plant, but not quite as water-sensitive. As you can see, a new version of the plant will eventually come poking out, as the old leaves slowly wither away. Below right: a nicely patterned conophytum.

Right: *Cheriodopsis candidissima*, blushing purple in the winter cold.

Left: An argyroderma in purple bloom.

Right: an unidentified mesemb that blooms annually in California.

Below left: 'Split Rock', *Pleiospilos nellii*, looks like a much larger version of a lithop, but is easier to grow and gets quite a bit larger. Below right: an unusual upright mesemb named *Smicrostigma viride* (although two members of the genus Ruschia, *R. crassa* and *R. uncinata*, both look remarkably similar.) I think there is still some reclassification to do here.

Left: a gaggle of *Gibbaeum heathii* appear to be mooning the photographer.

Below left: an unidentfied rock-type mesemb, possibly a species of gibbaeum, although it also could be a dinteranthus or something else entirely. You can authoritatively state a Latin name for one of these mystery plants and will very rarely be corrected. However, I speak often to cactus and succulent clubs, and I can't get a wild guess past them very easily. Every club has an expert on a particular type of succulent, including mesembs.

There are a couple of excellent books on mesembs, covering in several hundred pages a much more thorough examination of the group than I can do in a few pages here. My favorite is *Mesembs of the World* by Briza Press.

Above: *Delosperma echinatum* is a bushy plant with micro-fibers on its skin, with white to yellow flowers in season.

Above: *Glottiphyllum longum* or *G. linguiforme* are some of the more available of the ground-cover types. They have bright green, gumby-like leaves and large yellow flowers in fall and winter. They slowly crawl and cluster over an area, but not nearly as aggressive as the iceplant types, such as lampranthus. It is also apparently self-fertile, and I've noticed little seedlings sprouting in the vicinity of the larger plants. They tend to stay within a small footprint, so I wouldn't label them as invasive.

Below left: A mixed bowl of 'rock types', growing in a rock pocket. Center: *Titanopsis calcarea* is a small plant with very cool, reptilian style bumps on its leaves. Right: *Conophytum elishae* look like a gaggle of recently hatched alien baby birds waiting for a meal. Well, that's what I see. You can use your imagination with succulents.

Stapelia paniculata ssp. scitula
Photo: John Trager

Huernia reticulata
Photo: John Trager

One of the dirty tricks we succulent geeks like to pull is to have someone take a big whiff of the unusual starfish flowers of a stapeliad. Its a dirty trick because they really stink – one common name for the group is the 'carrion flower', because they can sometimes smell like rotten meat. They have opted out of the bee pool and decided to use flies as pollinators, hence the smell of rotting flesh. But you have to get real close to smell the very temporary flowers (but they will smell up an enclosed, hot and sunny room).

The primary types of stapeliads available are either from the genus stapelia, huernia or caralluma, but there are many other genera within the larger group, including orbea, hoodia, edithcolea, pseudolithos, and more. The plants are mostly nice little spineless, often fuzzy collections of small columns, but the attraction is really the diverse array of really cool and alien-looking flowers. They even look cool as puffed up pods a few days before they peel open. Among the largest flowers are *Stapelia gigantea* and *Stapelia grandiflora*, which can over time form substantial colonies in the landscape. Blooming time is typically fall into early winter.

There has been a lot of reclassification of all of these plants in the milkweed group, so be aware that old names may have changed. I may be using some old names here myself.

STAPELIADS

Stapilia grandiflora

Huernia variegata

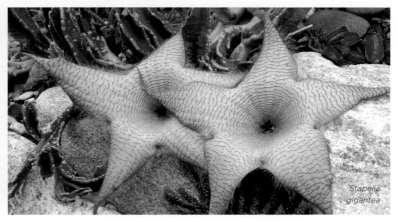

Stapelia gigantea

Calandrinia spectabilis (a.k.a. *Calendrinia grandiflora*, *Cistanthe grandiflora*), at left, is not exactly obscure. In fact it is quite common, but it sits by itself botanically in a rather obscure genus, of which *C. spectabilis* seen here is the only commonly seen representative. It is much loved for its' incandescent purple flowers that blow in the wind like purple poppies. It flowers quite a bit and the plant grows very fast – to the point of swallowing up many of its smaller neighbors. But that's not the real problem with this plant, which I seldom use anymore, as it looks good for a year or two, occupies a large space, but usually ends up getting leggy and then woody and then ugly – (see photo below) to the point that it needs to be cut out or at least severely trimmed, and it takes a while to bounce back. It is a beauty for a while, but be warned.

Below left : an excellent ground cover, *Othonna capensis*, sometimes called 'Little Pickles'.

Below right: *Bulbine caulescens* is an excellent landscape accent plant with yellow spring flowers. There is an orange flowered form as well.

Calandrinia spectabilis

Bulbine caulescens

Boophane distichia (pronounced 'Bo-ah-funy') is a highly coveted bulb succulent.

The next few pages are just a grab-bag attempt to show you a sample of some more soft succulents that don't fit into the major genera already sampled here. Some are succulent members of groups that might be primarily non-succulent, others are just obscure little oddities with very few members of its particular genus – but they all fit into the soft and succulent feel of the rest of the plants in this book. The category of 'succulent bulbs' below, for example, is pretty broad and nebulous (all 'bulbs' are pretty much succulent, but these bulbs are xerophytic plants from dry climates).

Succulent bulbs

There are thousands of annual bulb-type succulents, and many are hard to track down. Part of the reason may be because they disappear back to a bulb-only phase for part of the year, which can make them difficult to sell as a retail plant (its not dead, just dormant!). Inset above is 'Sea Squill', *Urginia maritima* (close up of seasonal flower to right).

One of the best of the bulb genera is the genus albuca, and the favorite of those has to be *Albuca spiralis*, seen below right. The species name accurately describes its growth habit, not to mention pretty lemon-lime striped flowers. At left is the 'Sea Onion', *Ornithogalum caudatum*. Below left is *Albuca* 'Augrabies Hills'.

Photo:
Tina Zucker

Hoya carnosa

Ceropegia

Ceropegias (above) are small, vining or scrambling plants, related to and somewhat resembling the hoyas, but most lack the thicker, waxy and larger leaves of the latter group. Most have tiny and elaborate little flowers that look a bit like lanterns. The most common form is the long-established 'Rosary Vine' or 'String of Hearts', *Ceropegia woodii*, with elaborate leaf patterns and a small caudex at the base of the vine. There is a nice white/pink variegated form as well.

Hoyas

These are primarily vining houseplant-looking plants from the milkweed family, and are usually considered succulents, despite being from tropical India and Southeast Asia. They handle much drier conditions because they are typically epiphytic, and have evolved thick, fleshy and waxy leaves to survive life in the trees. They also have wonderful clustering alien-looking waxy flowers.

Monanthes is a small genus of the crassulacea from the Canary Islands. The cute and fragile plant *Monanthes polyphylla*, is seen at left. If forms a small green carpet, with tiny yellowish flowers. It is an excellent plant to fill small pockets in rock scapes.

Monanthes polyphylla
Photo: Karen Zimmerman

Anacampseros telephiastrum – 'tricolor'

Right: A delightful miniature/ container plant, *Anacampseros telephiastrum* 'Tricolor' is a pretty, pink, low-grower.

Plectranthus

The genus plectranthus are warm weather plants of the mint family from sub-Saharan Africa, through India to Australia. Visually they seem to be more of a standard, bushy garden or houseplant, but a few can be considered more succulent in nature, and have some nice ornamental value. Many offer nice variegation, have intricate blue flowers, and most have a distinct smell, from minty to skunk-like.

The variegated plant at left might be *Plectranthus neochilus* 'Mike's Fuzzy Wuzzy'

Portulaca molokiniensis

Portulacas are new world plants, not related to portulacarias, although the name similarity is unfortunate. Most are ground-cover types with bright flowers, but haven't proven long-term hardy. The distinct species '*molokiniensis*', right, is indigenous to the tiny horseshoe crater island off of Maui, one of the few Hawaiian succulents in cultivation, along with *Brighamia insignis*.

Tradescantia

Tradescantias are New World herbaceous plants, some of which are also in the semi-succulent realm, being mostly sun-loving and xerophytic. The deep purple *T. pallida at* left is a favorite understory plant. Middle image appears to be *T. 'Greenlee'* ' and the right-hand images looks like the fuzzy *Tradescantia sillamontana*. Most have pleasing purple, pink or blueish flowers.

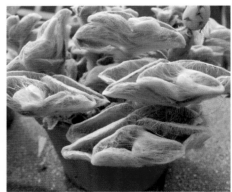

Adromischus

Adromischus are smallish tufting plants, related to cotyledon and tylecodon. Most are too small and sometimes frail to be considered landscape plants, but as you can see here, they can make fantastic container subjects. They bloom with small flowers on vertical stems. The most common in cultivation is likely *Adromischus cristatus*, above left. The two iterations of *A. marianae* above are prized collector plants.

Pepperomias

Pepperomias are indeed succulent members of the pepper family. The types in ornamental collections are typically very small South American plants, somewhat tropical and finicky in cultivation, but they have an undeniable appeal.

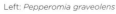

Left: *Pepperomia graveolens*

Right: *Pepperomia ?*

Sansevierias

Sansieverias, or at least a handful of them, have long been considered houseplants, but in fact most can be seen as soft succulents. Usually used as a potted plant, they can be used effectively in the landscape as well, providing an almost tropical feel. The various wide-bladed plants are most frequently encountered, particular *S. trifasciata* above right, but there are a handful of sharp and cylindrical forms that have a desert/architectural appeal. Flowers appear on vertical stems from the base of the plant, and are often sweetly fragrant.

Xercosicyos danguyi

Pedilanthus tithymaloides

Left: This round-leaved climber is also called the Penny Plant or the Silver Dollar Vine. It is a dry-climate vining plant from an arid part of Madagascar, with small spring yellowish flowers as seen here. It does best with climbing support, and once established can cover quite a bit of fence.

Right: Many of the plants in the genus pedilanthus have a more arid and stark appeal, similar to a number of desert euphorbias. There are a few that are more leafy and almost tropical in appearance, such as the variegated *P. tithymaloides*, seen at right, which comes in several different iterations.

283

Wow, you made it this far and are reading my closing notes? Thank you, you're my kind of reader. Wait, you're not the type that starts from the back are you? Well, however you got here, I hope you enjoyed the images and the words I squeezed in between them. This book has been a lot of fun to put together, and it was really hard to stop at my predetermined page count.

It is astounding how many appealing shapes and colors succulents have evolved into in their time on the planet. And they, or their probably equally beautiful forerunners, existed as gorgeous specimens of living art long before modern humans with any ability to appreciate them as such came about. Maybe some early mammal took a sidelong glance and thought 'that's cool'. And then took a bite, because what else were plants good for? Well, there's fixing carbon and providing oxygen and all that, and most serve an ecological purpose in their native habitat. But for us, they are beautiful representatives of glorious nature to keep in captivity as our little ornamental marvels. They make us happy. And of course we do what humans do – mess around with nature and conjure up new creatures that never would have existed without our help. By the time you read this, there will be a few more succulent novelties that will have hit the market.

Hunting down and photographing my favorite plants in their suburban habitat has become a bit of an addiction for me. Finding and photographing the softies for this book helped me transition from the aloe and agave images I had been collecting the previous few years for that book. My targets for the next book will be the spiny and sculptural euphorbias, cacti, and other desert icons that are also prominent players in California landscapes. I hope the spines won't scare you off – there are some amazing plants in that large and loosely defined category.

After working your way through this book, I hope you have a better handle on some of the plants you have or may have seen in your neighborhood. Go explore your local botanical garden, or just keep an eye out as you're cruising around town for all the succulents decorating residential and commercial areas. Some of these images here were taken just that way. I had to pull over, get out of the car, and snap a picture. A few I shot right out of the window. There is a succulent garden I walk past with my dog daily, planted long ago by the house's previous owner, that is just evolving wonderfully on its own with little apparent help from the new owner. Large clumps of Catlin aeoniums expand, contract, and bloom at various times of the year, an agave will occasionally bloom out, to be replaced by its pups – it is just a wonderful piece of introduced nature that is now doing its' thing by itself, appreciated by the few of us with the eye and inclination to watch it evolve. I do pull a few weeds every now and then.

Lastly, keep an eye out for the annual show and sale put on by your local cactus and succulent society – or better yet, join it. You'll meet a lot of happy and enthusiastic fellow nature lovers. And, I speak from experience here, support your local small or independent nursery. That is where you might find the rare or unusual plants you've been looking for. You need us and we need you!

INDEX